everyday heroes

CONTINUUM • NEW YORK

2000

The Continuum Publishing Company
370 Lexington Avenue
New York, N.Y. 10017

COPYRIGHT © 2000 BY PARADE PUBLICATIONS, INC.

Design by Ira Yoffe

Printed in Barcelona, Spain

Library of Congress Cataloging-in-Publication Data
Vittorini, Nancy.
Everyday heroes: stories of courage, compassion and conviction
from react, the magazine that raises teen voices / Nancy Vittorini.
p. cm.
Profiles originally published in the "everyday heroes" column of react magazine.
ISBN 0-8264-1217-3 (alk. paper)
1. Heroes—United States—Biography.
2. Teenagers— United States— Biography. I. Title.
CT220.V58 1999
920.073'0835— dc21
[B]   99-052161

Since

react magazine's debut in 1995, Nancy Vittorini has written a weekly column profiling young people who have made a significant difference in their communities and beyond. She calls them "everyday heroes," which is also, of course, the name of her column.

I am her editor. Thus I can share with you the certain knowledge that Nancy taps every possible resource—from news reports to organizations such as The Boys & Girls Clubs of America—to find these remarkable young people. Wherever she travels, she discovers teens who deserve to be celebrated—and stories that need to be told.

The "Everyday Heroes" feature has struck a responsive chord among **react**'s 4.5 million teen readers. For example, after Nancy profiled a girl who collected hats for young cancer patients, more than 3,000 **react** readers responded by contributing hats to the girl's cause. The column has inspired teens to join numerous organizations and to participate in everything from mentoring to disaster-relief efforts.

The column was also a catalyst for our creation of the annual **react** Take Action Awards. Each year, **react** and the New World Foundation grant hundreds of thousands of dollars in college scholarships and philanthropic prizes to the leading teen activists across the country.

Nancy's mission parallels that of **react** itself: to help young people get involved in the world and be heard. She helps teens identify and take action against the problems and injustices in their communities. The profiles in this book, each including their date of publication, are written with profound respect for the power and aspirations of America's young people. Taken together, they are a portrait of a generation that is banding together to create a better and more compassionate world.

Perhaps you'll find a way to help them. In fact, I know you will.

—Lee Kravitz
Editor, **react** magazine

sister act

Sixteen-year-old

Sisters doing it fo...

JULIE BIDWELL

Ta-Keesha White knows all about the tough times. She never got to know her father. And her mother suffers from a disease that makes it difficult to leave home, let alone work. So most of her life in Springfield, Mass., Ta-Keesha and her family have just scraped by.

But last year, Ta-Keesha's luck began to change. She won a scholarship to the prestigious Northfield Mount Hermon boarding school in Northfield, Mass. And now she's poised to become the first person in her family ever to go to college.

While most people would be content to chill out and enjoy the good times, Ta-Keesha says, "Since I have a full scholarship, I feel like I have to give something back." So she volunteered for her school's Big Sisters program.

Since last September, she's spent about two to three hours a week with 10-year-old Heidi Cyr, a fourth-grader at Northfield Elementary. Ta-Keesha says she knows how important it is to be a positive role model. Sometimes that just means hanging out with Heidi. At other times, it means being there to listen when Heidi needs her.

Heidi is living with her grandparents while her parents are sorting through family problems. "Sometimes Heidi needs to vent out all her problems and talk for hours," Ta-Keesha says. "I listen and let her know I've been through the same kind of problems—that I'm 16 and I've never had a conversation with my father. And I try to keep her feeling good about herself and tell her things will get better."

Has Heidi changed since becoming Ta-Keesha's little sis? "Yes! She's changed a

Lo gets ready for next week's 6-mile walk-a-thon.

DOUGLAS POKE

MAKING GREAT STRIDES

An Oklahoma teen raises thousands to combat cystic fibrosis.

When Lauren "Lo" Detrich

was just 3 months old, doctors told her parents that she would be lucky if she saw her 20th birthday. Lo was born with cystic fibrosis, a fatal lung and digestive disease.

But Lo, now 14, is a fighter. To control her illness, she takes 50 pills every day, and for three hours each day she uses two special machines that help her breathe. "Every breath of life is a prayer answered," Lo says.

Though medical treatment for cystic fibrosis has gotten better since she was a baby, and Lo now can expect to live to at least age 30, she is doing whatever she can

"E... y... to... s... gi... m... ba... pe...

to ra...

S... Cys... Grea... the... coll... been... year... Lo,... fund... last... $50...

Lo... the l... prom... $20,... coll... dred... in th... to t... even...

nam... walk... held... Lo a... scho... parti...

Lo... Mon... in T... spok... and t... need...

"I... bette... do it without help. Every minute you give to helping someone with cystic fibrosis is like giving a minute of life back to that person."

—*Nancy Vittorini*

TIM HALE

A 10-minute walk helped Richie Hiatt earn thousands of dollars for families of children with cancer.

walking tall

For his Eagle Scout project, Richie Hiatt, 14, of Los Alamitos, Calif., decided to raise money to help families of children with cancer. He thought he could raise $500 or maybe even $1,000 at best. But when he later learned that his own 7-year-old sister was diagnosed with leukemia, his ambitions for the project grew.

"I saw Laci suffer through the chemotherapy," Richie says. "I saw her throw up, and I saw her hair fall out." Motivated by his sister's struggle, he spent seven months planning his fund-raiser, Walk On for a Cure for Cancer. Richie wanted it to take place at Los Alamitos High School, where he will be a freshman this fall. He made the walk short—a quarter-mile around the school track—because his sister wanted to walk the entire distance herself, despite the pain it would cause her. "If my sister couldn't walk the whole walk, I would carry her," Richie says.

Richie received support from his Boy Scout troop, church, school and business groups. Newspapers and TV stations publicized the event

> **"If my sister couldn't walk the whole walk, I would carry her."**

throughout the Los Angeles area.

Then, on a spring day last year, more than 200 people arrived at the high school track. As the theme from *Rocky* played, Richie led the walk with Laci, who had been in the hospital with a fever only the day before. Two cancer patients joined them, and other teens with cancer showed up to lend their encouragement as well.

The walk took only 10 minutes, but it generated donations for almost a year. Richie's walk eventually raised almost $16,000.

Richie sent the money to Parents Against Cancer, a nonprofit organization in Long Beach, Calif., which helps kids with cancer whose parents have limited financial resources. The money is being used for costly medications, checkups, transportation to hospitals or clinics, refrigerators to store medicines—even wigs for teens who have lost their hair.

"If you believe in yourself and your cause, others will too," Richie says. And Laci, now 8, is doing fine. Her cancer is in remission.

—*Nancy Vittorini*

Over

the past four years, **react** magazine has given me the opportunity to interview some of our country's most outstanding young people for its "Everyday Heroes" column, which recognizes ordinary teens who are doing something truly extraordinary. Some of these young people have won medals and received honors for their actions. Others have been selected as **react** Take Action Award winners. *All* are heroes whose efforts have inspired and empowered millions of other **react** readers. Within these pages, you'll meet a few of these "everyday heroes" and find within them measures of courage, compassion and conviction.

Courage can be found in those heroes who placed themselves in harm's way to help another, like Justin Havlik, who used his high school wrestling experience to stop a burglary and subdue an armed robber. Or Tiare Marie Wells, who pulled a man from the icy waters of a frozen reservoir. Or Tim Krieger, who risked his life to rescue a stranger from a burning car. "Anyone would have done it," Tim told me.

Then there's the courage—and conviction—of Lauren Detrich, who was born with cystic fibrosis. "Every breath of life is a prayer answered," she said. Despite having to use two machines daily to help her breathe, Lauren worked tirelessly as a spokesperson and fund-raiser for the Cystic Fibrosis Foundation. Michael Higgins has an equally compelling cause—to teach his peers about the risks of cigarette smoking. And Rachael Tanker's commitment to raise awareness about human-rights injustices in Nigeria took a global vision. "I want to do something to stop people from being killed unjustly in the future," Rachael told me. "Everyone deserves a fair trial and fair punishment."

The compassion of these young people for others is the thread that binds the stories. Many devote their time and energy toward raising much-needed funds, like Richie Hiatt, who created a walk-a-thon to help families of children with cancer, and Brooke Lyons, who organized a benefit ballet performance to help raise awareness about scoliosis, a condition she herself suffers from. Others show their compassion for animals, like Molly Vandewater, who turned her home into a wildlife refuge for injured animals.

Whether it be through courage, compassion or conviction, teens throughout the world are changing our future and positively influencing others to do the same. Every week I have the joy of writing about them. When I ask each one what he or she would like our 4.5 million teen readers to know, the responses are similar. Tell them to get involved, they say. And stand up for what you believe in. And that it doesn't matter that you're young, you can still do something to make the world a better place. Each conversation with one of our "heroes" reminds me of an anonymous quote: "If you think you're too small to make a difference, you've never been in bed with a mosquito." Young people have passion and they have power. Read their stories, and you, too, will be inspired.

—**Nancy Vittorini**

*It may come in risking their lives
to save another's life, or in facing
a life that's filled with risk.
Courage comes in many forms but has
the same ingredient for these teens:
a brave spirit to respond to
danger and difficulty, often
without even thinking about it.*

courage

It was a cold night in February of last year. Logan Johnson, then 17, was delivering pizza in Dallas when he saw a Cadillac veer off a road and plunge into a deep pond. Logan had only one thought: "Whoever is in that car, I'm going to get them out."

With great difficulty, Logan pulled out the driver—a 65-year-old minister who had lost consciousness behind the wheel—before the car sank. Logan brought him to the shore and safety. By then, a crowd had gathered and pulled them both out of the water.

Logan credits the incident with saving his own life.

"Just two weeks before it all happened," he says, "I had attempted suicide. I was having a lot of personal and family problems and had dropped out of school, thinking I could make it better on my own. But [I realized] it doesn't work that way. I was working two jobs 80 hours a week and still barely making it. Saving the reverend put a whole different perspective on my life and helped me to understand the value of life itself."

Last summer, Logan returned to school and is now a senior at J.J. Pearce High in a Dallas suburb. After graduation, he plans to join the Marine Corps Reserves, then head for college in the fall.

"This was a wake-up call for me," he says. "My goal now is to share my story—to talk with other teens and encourage them to stay in school. When people say a high school diploma opens up doors, they're not lying. It really does. When things are tough, don't drop out. Stick in there."

Logan was awarded the prestigious Carnegie Medal in December. The medal is given to those from the United States and Canada who risk their lives to an extraordinary degree while saving or attempting to save the lives of others.

PUBLISHED IN **react** ON MARCH 25, 1996
DALLAS, TEXAS

logan johnson

Last

fall, 17-year-old Tim Krieger and a friend were walking a dog in Moundsview, Minn. They weren't expecting anything more dramatic than a quick cleanup with a pooper-scooper. But just as they were about to cross a street, a car that stopped to let them pass was rammed from behind by another driver. It spun 360 degrees and stopped on the other side of the intersection.

Tim learned later that the driver who crashed into the car had gone into shock from a medical condition and stepped on the accelerator by accident.

At first, Tim says, he and his friend stood there stunned. Then sparks from the crash lit a trail of gas like a fuse leading to the car that was hit.

Tim ran over and tried to open the driver's door. But it wouldn't budge. Fire had already spread beneath the car, and flames surrounded it. Tim saw the driver, Kenneth Lease, slouched in the front seat.

Jumping over the flames, Tim tried the passenger door, which was jammed. "By that time, I was getting pretty frustrated," Tim says. "And my friend was yelling at me to get out of there. I knew I was going to get fried if I didn't hurry."

Tim finally forced the door open. While flames spread to the back seat, he dragged Lease to the side of the road. About 15 seconds later, the car exploded.

When the police arrived, Tim went home. It wasn't until he called to check on Lease's condition that the police learned of Tim's bravery.

For his heroism, Tim was honored by the Moundsview Police Department. And he was awarded a 1995 Carnegie Medal, given to people who risk their lives while attempting to save others.

Would he do the same thing again? Sure, Tim says. "I really didn't think that much of it then…and I don't now. Anybody would have done it."

JULY 1, 1996, MOUNDSVIEW, MINN.

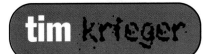
tim krieger

11

Best friends Louis Pechaver, left, and Eric Jones helped rescue two men.

When

a tropical storm hit their hometown of Jacksonville, Fla., best friends Louis Pechaver and Eric Jones didn't have time to get scared—two men's lives depended on them.

Louis and Eric were on their way home from school and barely had been able to pull out of the flooded parking lot at Wolfson High. But it wasn't long before their car stalled on the road in the rising waters. As they tried to get the car started again, the two friends heard cries for help. A man was trapped in his car, which was sinking in a flooded ditch nearby, and another man was trying to get him out. Louis and Eric told the man in the car to get into the back seat, then the other man broke a window so the three of them could pull him out.

"But then it got really scary," Louis says. "As we were pulling the passenger out, the car started to sink really fast. The suction was pulling the other guy down. Eric and I grabbed him for dear life." The car ended up sinking, but both men were saved by Eric and Louis, who say they just followed their instincts.

"When we saw someone needed help, we just ran on pure impulse, never thinking that anything bad would happen to us," Louis remembers. "My only fear was that I might have seen someone get hurt or die." The local newspaper recognized Eric and Louis for their efforts in the storm, which occurred in late 1994. They are both 19 now and plan to attend college this fall.

JANUARY 1, 1996, JACKSONVILLE, FLA.

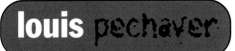

louis pechaver

AND

eric jones

The robber

was armed with what looked like a gun wrapped in newspaper. He seemed high on drugs. He ordered Marlene Fernandez to give him the key to her hair salon's cash register. Shaking, Fernandez struggled to find the key on one of the three keychains she carried. Her delay gave Justin Havlik, 19, the opening he needed: He emerged from behind a wall, grabbed the robber's wrist and arm and threw him to the floor.

Justin, a freshman at Marymount Manhattan College, was getting his hair washed in the the back of the Dramatics salon in New York City last December when the thief burst in. "I knew I had to do something," he says. "I kept thinking that the woman behind the register could have been my mother or my girlfriend. If the guy had blown her head off in front of me, I would have had to live with that for the rest of my life."

Justin was on the wrestling team at Xavier High School in New York City and also had some boxing experience. But he was surprised by the strength of the man he tackled. "He was about 5-foot-5 and 130 pounds or so. Not a big guy, but determined to get out of there. We were behind the cash register in a confined space, so when he stood up, I blocked him and threw him against a wall," Justin says.

The "gun" turned out to be a pipe wrapped in newspaper. As Justin grappled with the thief, one of the salon employees called the police.

"He clawed at me and yelled for me to let him go," Justin says. He admits he was frightened, "but I had to stop someone from doing something that was extremely wrong. I had to repress my fear because when you're acting in fear, you're not in control. When I pushed it aside, it gave me the ability to take action. What I did came out of my heart."

When the police arrived, Justin asked them to be kind to the suspect, whom police say has a record dating back 14 years for drug possession and theft. "I felt sorry for him," Justin says. "To go to those extremes, you have to be desperate. Problems in life can turn you to the breaking point. But that doesn't mean what he did was right. He has to face the consequences. And he's going to get what he deserves."

Police always strongly advise bystanders not to try to stop thieves who may be armed and dangerous. Justin says the officers arriving at the hair salon commended him for his handling of the situation, but, he says, "they said they don't suggest it."

justin havlik

MARCH 2, 1998, NEW YORK, N.Y.

photograph by dennis curran/sports file

16

It was 10:15 at night when Graham Budd, a Civil Air Patrol cadet, got a phone call. A small four-seater plane traveling from Canada to Massachusetts was declared missing. Graham, 14, and the seven other members of his squadron were asked by the U.S. Air Force to help find the plane and any survivors.

Graham was no stranger to emergency work. Through the Civil Air Patrol, a volunteer civilian branch of the Air Force that provides emergency services, Graham had taken classes in wilderness hiking, radio communication and electronic direction-finding. He joined the cadet program after taking his first flying lesson in seventh grade.

The Vermont teen and his team, which included four other teens, headed out in a van to find the crash site. To locate the plane, they used a radio tracking device, which received the emergency signals from the plane's transmitter.

The signals pointed toward a mountain in southern Vermont, three hours away from where Graham's team had started. The nearby New York state police were helping to scope out the area with their helicopter. "They could search from the sky much faster," Graham explains.

Graham's team worked all through the night, hoping to find survivors. At dawn, the helicopter spotted the crash site. When the team reached the summit, they discovered no one had survived. "Our job was over," Graham says. Exhausted and sad, he returned home to South Burlington, determined to continue his rescue work.

Though the mission last fall ended in tragedy, other efforts to help have been more successful.

During an ice storm last year, Graham's squadron ran a Red Cross program to provide shelter information. "One woman called us her guardian angels," Graham says. "Without us, these people wouldn't have had food every morning or a place to be. It's a really, really great feeling to see the results of your work."

OCTOBER 12, 1998, SOUTH BURLINGTON, VT.

graham budd

It started as a quiet spring break day. Two years ago, Tiare Marie Wells, a Colorado State University freshman, was sightseeing with two friends in Cody, Wyo. Then the quiet of the morning was shattered.

"We saw a man icefishing," Tiare says, "and wanted to take a closer look." The friends walked onto a frozen reservoir to chat with the fisherman. Meanwhile, two other trout fishermen, Charles Norwood and Blakes Powell, arrived and drilled their own fishing hole in the 3-inch-thick ice. But suddenly the ice beneath the men cracked, and one fell into the 38-degree water. Trying to pull his friend out, the second man also fell in and began calling for help.

Tiare and her friends, already on their way back to shore, heard the cries and saw Monte Bassett, 77, the man they had just met, rush over to help. Bassett almost had one of the men out of the water when he, too, fell in.

Tiare reacted quickly. She remembered that there was a horse halter and rope in the back of her car. Tiare hollered to a friend to throw them to her and then ran back to the ice hole. All three men's heads were still above water, but they were struggling to stay afloat. Tiare threw the halter to them, got down on her knees and started pulling.

"It didn't go through my head that I'd fall in, too," she says. "I just reacted to them needing help.

"Monte caught the halter, and the other two men held onto him. But they were so cold, they couldn't keep hold of his body," Tiare says. "They kept going under."

But Tiare kept pulling. "I don't know where I got the strength. I just kept pulling and pulling, and the strength came to me," she says. "Monte was holding onto the halter for dear life and kept telling me to keep pulling."

Finally, Tiare pulled Bassett out. She threw the halter back into the water, even though she could no longer see the other men's heads above the ice. But there was no tug at the other end of the lifeline—Norwood and Powell had drowned.

Meanwhile, Tiare's friends had flagged down a car whose driver used a cellular phone to call for help. For two hours, a rescue team searched for the two men's bodies. Eventually they were found, 25 feet under.

"I felt helpless I couldn't do anything more," says Tiare, now 20. But she had saved one grateful man's life, and for that she was awarded a 1997 Carnegie Medal for Extraordinary Heroism.

MAY 11, 1998, CODY, WYO.

tiare marie wells

19

photograph by casey ressler

Crispin Gentry, left, with Max
Talbert after the rescue.

It was zero degrees on a November afternoon in 1996 in Palmer, Alaska when Crispin Gentry, then 13, began looking for his friend, Max Talbert. Max, then 9, was supposed to be working on a snow fort in a neighbor's yard, but Crispin couldn't find him.

Then, Crispin says, "from a distance, I saw what I thought was a hat on top of a snow fort." As he got closer, Crispin realized it was someone's feet sticking straight up from the top of the fort.

"The first thing I thought was that someone was playing a joke," Crispin says. But then he saw that it was Max. While digging a hole at the top of the snow fort to hide from oncoming snowballs, Max had fallen in headfirst and gotten stuck.

"I tickled him, and when I didn't get a response, I thought he might be dead," Crispin says. Crispin acted quickly. He grabbed Max's legs and tried hard to pull him out. When that didn't work, Crispin picked up the plastic shovel that Max had used for building his snow fort and started digging.

"I dug in parallel to his body so I wouldn't hit him, and that released some snow," Crispin says. "Then I was able to pull him out."

Max was unconscious, his face blue and his body quivering. "Max coughed a couple of times, and I tilted his head back to make it easier for him to breathe," Crispin says. "But I had to get him home, fast."

Crispin managed to carry Max home. He helped Max's mother get him out of his wet clothes and wrap blankets around him. Crispin took the keys to Max's mother's truck and warmed up the engine so she could get her son to the hospital fast. There, Max was treated for hypothermia.

The doctor who took care of Max said if Crispin had not acted immediately, the boy may not have survived. Now a sophomore at Palmer High School, Crispin, 15, believes "some of the training I'd had in Boy Scouts told me what to do. And what the whole experience did," he says, "is remind me how precious life is and how easily it can slip away."

DECEMBER 28, 1998, PALMER, ALASKA

crispin gentry

Clinton

Brown may be only 3 feet 3 inches tall, but he's not short on self-confidence. Positive attitude rules in Clinton's life, even though the 14-year-old from Long Island, N.Y., was born with a form of dwarfism called diastrophic dysplasia.

"You gotta shoot for the stars," says Clinton, who hosted the TV documentary *Walk a Mile in My Shoes*. He won a New York Emmy for his part in the 1993 film, which explored the world through the eyes of disabled kids.

Clinton says disabled people have as much to offer the world as anyone else, and his own life serves as proof. He's endured 24 surgeries for his back and other problems, and he still manages to pursue his biggest passion—sports.

He loves all sports, but hockey comes first. Clinton has collected 150 hockey sticks, and he puts them to use playing center for the Henry Viscardi High School for Disabled Children in Albertson, N.Y. In January, his team got to face off against the New York Islanders, who played at the school in wheelchairs. The floor-hockey game ended in an 11-11 tie, and Clinton led all scorers. "I got three goals and one assist," he says as he recalls playing against his heroes. "The players are an inspiration to me—they make me feel good about myself."

Clinton, in turn, is an inspiration to others. He is a junior ambassador for the New York State Games for the Physically Challenged, where he's won 30 medals in track and field.

Clinton wants to become a sports reporter. "With my mind and my attitude," he says, "I think I can get pretty far." Who would bet against him?

J U N E   3 ,   1 9 9 6 ,   L O N G   I S L A N D ,   N . Y .

clinton brown

Clinton Brown, center, with one of his 150 hockey sticks and other players from his neighborhood.

photograph by todd france

Dennis "Boomer" Burns, right, with friend Paul Bucchieri and dog CR, in front of the Connecticut River in Windsor, Conn., where the boys found CR.

photograph by julie bidwell

Dennis

"Boomer" Burns and two of his friends were hanging out by the boat ramp in Windsor, Conn., one day last winter.

As they competed to see who could throw a rock the farthest, they saw something floating in the icy river. Boomer quickly realized it was a dog.

A strong current carried the dog rapidly from shore. Boomer and his buddies ran along the icy edge, hoping the dog would drift toward them. "He was looking at us," remembers Boomer, "and he was trying to bark but couldn't because his mouth was frozen shut."

Finally, the dog floated close enough for Boomer to crawl out on the ice and grab him. "He was too tired to get up on his own," says 14-year-old Boomer.

"We rubbed his legs and body to get his circulation going and then let him down to run beside us," Boomer recalls. The weary dog collapsed after a half-mile. So Boomer carried the 50-pound pit bull the rest of the way home.

Boomer was allowed to adopt his newfound friend and named him "CR," after the Connecticut River. "I take care of him, feed him, take him for walks and teach him tricks. He's pretty much my best buddy now."

In addition to being recognized for his heroic rescue by the Windsor Town Council, Boomer won the grand prize in a "Be Kind to Animals" contest sponsored by Strays and Others Inc., of New Canaan, Conn., a volunteer, nonprofit organization that helps place homeless animals with families.

OCTOBER 30, 1995, WINDSOR, CONN.

dennis burns

When

she started feeling sick to her stomach in March 1997, Tiffany Culy figured it was the flu. But a few days later, the Saline, Mich., teen woke up with yellow eyes and yellow skin and an "unbelievable pain" in her belly. Rushed to a hospital, she began slipping into a coma.

Tiffany had Wilson's disease, which was destroying her liver. Doctors said she would die without an immediate liver transplant.

After reviewing four possible organ donations, surgeons were able to find a liver that would work for her. Tiffany spent three months in the hospital. Now 19 and a freshman at Hope College in Holland, Mich., Tiffany is so healthy that she competed in two swimming events at the 1998 Transplant Games. She also has become a crusader for organ donations.

"Over 61,000 Americans are waiting for a lifesaving organ transplant," Tiffany says. And an average of 12 Americans die each day waiting for a new liver, heart, kidney or other organ, according to the nonprofit Coalition for Donation.

Tiffany gives talks at schools and to youth groups, telling kids that needing an organ can happen to anyone. "It took me totally by surprise," she says.

Tiffany tries to dispel myths about organ donation. For example, she says celebrities are not put at the top of the list for donations. "And there is no black market for stolen organs."

Tiffany says she got a liver because "I was basically healthy, and my chances for survival were good." When deciding who gets an organ, the coalition says it does not take into account race, gender, age, income or celebrity.

Becoming a donor is simple, Tiffany says. "All you really have to do is tell your next of kin, because that's who will be asked at the time of death. You can also sign up when you get your driver's license."

And you shouldn't wait. "Even though you're a teen, you're not invincible," she says. "Talk to your family. Tell them you want to save someone's life."

FEBRUARY 8, 1999, SALINE, MICH.

photograph by lynden steele

Joshua

and Jenny Gallegos didn't know any better. The happy toddlers, ages 20 months and 3 years, were playing on the train tracks across the street from their house in Merced, Calif., oblivious to the danger they were in. Their neighbor, 17-year-old Joe Terry, was just as happy sitting on his porch, listening to his Walkman. Luckily, even though Joe is deaf in one ear and the music was blasting, he could hear the piercing whistles and feel the strong vibrations that signal an oncoming train. He looked up and saw Jenny and Josh.

The adrenaline was pumping as Joe sprang off his chair and started running. As he slipped off his headphones, he heard people yelling from their cars: "Get off the tracks! A train's coming!" Joe raced across four lanes of traffic. "I wasn't thinking about anything except saving those kids' lives," Joe remembers.

With his eyes locked on the girl, he brushed past the boy, knocking him off the track to safety. He beelined to Jenny and scooped her up in his arms. Seconds later, the train rushed past at 60 mph, blowing Joe's baseball hat right off his head.

His heart still racing, Joe brought the kids back to their house, then headed home to tell his parents what happened.

Meanwhile, the train's conductor, who witnessed the whole event, made an emergency stop to report the incident. It wasn't long before everyone in town knew that Joe was a hero.

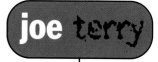

"I didn't feel like a hero at the time," Joe says, thinking back to the August 1995 rescue. "It felt more like a dream."

M ARCH 31 , 1997 , M ERCED , C ALIF .

photograph by thor swift

'The

flames didn't get me, but the heat sure did." This is how Daniel Lopez-Galvan remembers his lifesaving action in California.

Daniel, now 19, was driving his mother and two brothers home to La Cañada, Calif., from his grandmother's on Thanksgiving weekend in 1995. The traffic was racing by at 70 mph or faster on Highway 46 near San Luis Obispo.

Daniel was traveling behind an RV that swerved into oncoming traffic and plowed head-on into a pickup and a Volvo.

"When they hit, it was like an explosion," remembers Daniel. He pulled off the road and ran to help.

"I bolted across the highway and saw the pickup was completely inside the RV…all you could see was the bed of the truck sticking out." Both were in flames.

"The Volvo had rolled several times and come to a stop on its roof. The driver and passenger in the front seat were crushed, but I looked in the back seat and saw a girl's blond hair hanging down," he says.

He reached inside the broken window, struggling to release the child's seat belt. Gasoline poured from the Volvo's tank and pooled around Daniel's feet. He heard his mother screaming as the flames closed in, but he couldn't leave the girl. Finally, he grabbed her ankles, pulled her through the window and carried her to safety.

Before Daniel could help the other passengers, the car burst into flames. The girl, 8, survived the crash, but the rest of her family, including her 11-year-old sister, died.

After the rescue, Daniel was treated for second-degree burns to his left arm. He says the experience made him "a more careful driver and much more aware of how suddenly things can go wrong."

Would he try the same rescue again?

"Sure would…without thinking about it."

APRIL 21, 1997, LA CAÑADA, CALIF.

daniel lopez-galvan

31

They believe they have a responsibility toward one another and to making the world a better place. These teens channel their energy into doing things that are powerful, positive and good.

conviction

Ben

Smilowitz has been watching the world very carefully. The struggles of teens in his own community have made him realize that teens around the country "have no say." Ben has decided to do something about it.

Today, this 16-year-old from West Hartford, Conn., is the founder of the International Student Activism Alliance, which focuses on informing students about issues concerning them and gives them a chance to speak out. With 70 chapters now active in 18 states, the heart of ISAA is its member-written newsletter.

"A lot of students think their voice doesn't matter," Ben explains, "but it should." Especially, he believes, when it comes to issues such as the "zero-tolerance" policy gaining popularity in school districts. This means schools will not tolerate students who break any rules—from dress-code violations to carrying a weapon—and they are suspended without getting a hearing.

Ben is not alone in his fight. The Connecticut chapter of the American Civil Liberties Union not only supports him but also helps him with expenses.

"I'm trying to show that zero-tolerance policies are unconstitutional," Ben says, "since they don't let students tell their side of the story. Some think we're trying to loosen punishment," he adds, "but that's not it at all."

Other issues the ISAA is taking on are the right of students to serve on school boards, rights for learning-disabled students and ways of combating teenage drunken driving.

Ben's goal? "I'd like to have every student who wants to voice his or her opinion be a part of us."

MAY 12, 1997, WEST HARTFORD, CONN.

ben smilowitz

Valerie Edwards, left, and Erin Scheide took on a flawed Maryland law and changed it.

photograph by skip brown

In October of 1993, sixth-graders Cassie Weitzen, Valerie Edwards and Annie Davis sat giggling in the back seat of the van that Annie's mother was driving. Suddenly, a pickup truck broadsided them, sending them over an embankment. The three girls were rushed to intensive-care facilities.

According to police, the driver of the pickup told an officer that he'd been drinking beer, but he refused to take a blood alcohol test. Maryland law at that time allowed him to say no because no one had died at the scene.

By the next day, Annie Davis was dead of her injuries.

Today, Valerie and friend Erin Scheide, both 15, look back on that accident as a turning point in their lives. "Valerie had just lost her best friend," says Erin, who was not in the accident but says she made up her mind to be there for Valerie.

Soon after the accident, Valerie and Erin and the friends and family of Annie Davis formed a group called "For the Love of Annie." They dedicated themselves to changing the law that allowed drivers to refuse a blood alcohol test at an accident when there was no immediate fatality.

For eight years, similar bills had been failing to pass. And studies showed that more and more Maryland drivers were refusing to take the tests, making it harder to punish drivers for fatalities they might have caused.

"It seemed that the laws were protecting the drunken drivers instead of the victims," Valerie says. "We were determined to change that."

They created fliers and packets and faxed letters all over the state. They went knocking on legislators' doors, lobbying for their cause with every member of the Maryland House and Senate who would see them. They personally spent hours testifying, never letting anyone forget Annie.

To the surprise of many, the bill passed unanimously on April 5, 1994, less than seven months after the accident that took Annie's life.

Valerie and Erin continue their work in Annie's memory. Now ninth-graders at Severn River Junior High, they co-founded two active chapters of SADD (Students Against Drunk Driving), are involved in the Maryland Underage Drinking Prevention Coalition and speak at conferences.

Their message? "There's no excuse for anyone to get behind the wheel of a car if they've been drinking," Valerie says. "Tougher laws are needed."

JUNE 2, 1997, ARNOLD, MD

valerie edwards

AND

erin scheide

While

in her freshman year at Grant High School in Portland, Ore., Jennifer Fletcher was in a student production of *Oliver.* And she looked forward to being in more plays. But when she returned to school the next year, Jennifer learned that Grant had cut back its musical theater program.

Jennifer, now 16, says students had been warned that funds for arts programs were shrinking. "But when we were told we couldn't produce a play, it really hit me," she says.

Jennifer was also struck by the similarities between her school's situation and the 1995 movie *Mr. Holland's Opus.* The movie—about a school that loses its music program—had been filmed at Grant High. In it, Richard Dreyfuss plays a teacher who tries to save his school's arts program. And now Jennifer was struggling to do the same.

For a sophomore year English project, Jennifer wrote about how to produce a benefit concert. Then she made it happen. She wrote a letter explaining the situation to singer Jackson Browne. She knew he had performed at benefit concerts in the past and hoped he'd be willing to help.

Months went by without a response. Then, in June, she came home to find a message on her answering machine: "Jennifer, this is Jackson Browne."

"I was jumping and screaming," she says.

Later that evening, Browne called back, and Jennifer made her case. "I told him that the arts are a way for students to find out who they are. They're an alternative to drugs and alcohol. And for some, they're an incentive to stay in school."

It was enough to convince Browne. In October, he performed before a sellout crowd of 2,700 at a Portland concert hall. The show raised $100,000.

Jennifer used the money to help create Arts Alive, an arts fund for all 98 of Portland's public schools. She hopes some of the money will help pay for two musicals at Grant High next year.

"It sounds corny, but it's true," says Jennifer, who was honored in November with the statewide Governor's Arts Award. "If you believe in something, you can achieve it. But you have to work for it."

jennifer fletcher

FEBRUARY 22, 1999, PORTLAND, ORE.

Jackson Browne with Jennifer Fletcher, right, and her sister, Sarah.

Laotian

immigrants who now live in San Francisco carried their traditions with them when they came to the United States, including a lifestyle centered on fishing. But when 16-year-old Sipfou Saechao (SIP-foo SAY-chow) of San Pablo, Calif., learned of pollution in the waters where the community fished, she had to speak out.

Pollution has contaminated San Francisco Bay with high levels of poisons that infect fish and could endanger people who eat the catch. Last summer, Sipfou and other summer interns working with the Asian Pacific Environmental Network researched the problem, discovered that the pollution most directly affected the Laotian community, and then took the issue to the community's leaders.

Sipfou's message was important because there is no way to tell that the fish are polluted by sight or taste. Warning signs posted near fishing spots are in English, which more than half of Laotian immigrants cannot read. Sipfou, who came to the United States in 1984, joined others who speak both languages to explain the environmental dangers and to teach neighbors how to prepare fish in ways that reduce the risk from the poisons.

"Our elders got a chance to learn how we feel and understand that we are serious," says Sipfou, who continues to speak to local students about protecting the environment.

For her work, Sipfou, a junior at Richmond High School in Richmond, Calif., was named a runner-up in last year's **react** Take Action Awards. She has divided the prize—$25,000 of merchandise for needy children—among three groups: Downer Elementary School, where she has tutored since she was in eighth grade; her school's Adolescent Parent Program, which assists pregnant teens and teen parents; and a program that provides homeless students at Richmond with clothes and school supplies.

"Some of my friends are homeless and in the program," Sipfou says. "I complain sometimes about what I don't have, and then I think about them and I see that I take things for granted."

OCTOBER 20, 1997, SAN PABLO, CALIF.

sipfou saechao

Sipfou and some of the
children benefiting from the
strollers that were part of
her Take Action Award prize.

When

he was 13 and on his school's track and soccer teams, Seth Ginsberg started having trouble sprinting and climbing steps. Growing pains, he was told. But he never grew out of them.

Soon he was diagnosed with arthritis—a disease that causes pain and swelling in the joints. Seth's type of arthritis affects his back, knees and his left hand.

Seth, now 17, of Spring Valley, N.Y., says, "Even with medicine, it's hard. In the mornings my joints are stiff. Often I have to crawl to the bathroom."

He says he's frustrated because most people don't associate arthritis with kids—they think it's something only grandparents get. "Even some school nurses don't understand it," he says.

But almost 300,000 young people in the United States suffer from this disease, according to the Arthritis Foundation.

"It can be just as bad or worse for kids," Seth says. "An adult may not be able to play as much tennis as he wants. I wouldn't even be able to grip the racket."

Seth wants to make more people aware of juvenile arthritis, so he spends every free moment volunteering at his local Arthritis Foundation. He began two years ago by stuffing envelopes. Now he is writing press releases, speaking at fund-raisers, counseling kids and working on a Web site with information for young people with arthritis.

Seth believes it's important that kids learn as much as they can about the disease. "Children with arthritis are in pain. If kids were diagnosed earlier," he says, "symptoms wouldn't get so advanced, and it would be easier to relieve the pain."

A senior at Rockland Country Day School, Seth was honored last summer by the Arthritis Foundation for his volunteer work. He also was the only teen named to his local foundation's advisory board. And he wants to do more.

"It's a lonely and scary place for young people who suffer," Seth says. "I will spearhead the effort until it brings arthritis to its knees."

MARCH 15, 1999, SPRING VALLEY, N.Y.

seth ginsberg

When

retired Gen. Colin Powell fielded questions from hundreds of reporters at the Presidents' Summit for America's Future last March, he didn't face any reporters quite like 15-year-old Becky Jarvis of Minneapolis.

Becky was one of 10 teens covering the meeting in Philadelphia for the Summit Action Youth Web site (www.americaspromise.org). And when she saw an opportunity to talk to Powell, who chaired the national conference on volunteering, she grabbed it.

"He was sitting two rows ahead of me in one of the sessions," Becky says. "I silently slipped to the end of the row he was sitting in, and as the lights came up and he stood to leave, I was the first reporter to catch his attention.

"His press agent told me he didn't have time for an interview," Becky says. But she argued, "This is a question from the youth at the summit."

That convinced Powell. He guided Becky through the crowd, and as they walked, surrounded by bodyguards, Becky started asking questions.

She told him she represented more than 250 youth leaders at the summit and that "some of them felt like spectators. I asked him if youth were there just to be talked to or to take a leadership role. He admitted that youth had not been part of the process as much as they could have been."

Powell wasn't the only politician who came face to face with Becky in Philadelphia. She asked California Gov. Pete Wilson if he thought the push for volunteering was needed to help people hurt by cuts in welfare programs in states like his. "He basically dodged the question," she says. The Rev. Jesse Jackson told Becky that another national summit was needed to address the issue of inequality in the United States.

Back home, Becky continues to work toward the summit's goal of increasing the number of Americans, especially teens, who commit their time to volunteering. Already a member of Minnesota's Youth Advisory Council, a group of teens that advises the state government on youth issues, she also was one of only two high school students added to a state commission planning a similar summit next May.

When they talked about a national volunteer movement, Powell told Becky, "We can make it happen." She has already begun.

JULY 21, 1997, MINNEAPOLIS, MINN.

becky jarvis

photograph by dan monick

photograph by tim hale

46

When

he was a boy, Jacob Green's grandparents told him of their experiences during World War II, stories he'll never forget: His grandfather escaped from Germany, then returned with the U.S. Army to fight the Nazis. His grandmother survived a Nazi concentration camp. Those family memories, says Jacob, now 18, "helped me grow up with very strong feelings about promoting tolerance and fighting hate."

Those feelings would be put to the test in his hometown of Los Alamitos, Calif. While Jacob was in eighth grade, the town's high school was rocked by an act of hate: Vandals stuffed racist and anti-Semitic material into lockers and spray-painted swastikas on the building.

"I was horrified," Jacob says, and he resolved to do something about it. That fall, as a freshman at Los Alamitos High, he joined Griffins With a Mission. The club was formed after the vandalism to bring students together at day-long retreats to face and overcome their differences. (The griffin is the Los Alamitos High mascot.)

Jacob was trained to lead retreat activities, including one game in which a paper plate is hung behind each student's neck. Written on the plate is a description—"African-American," "Hispanic," "surfer." As the student circles the room, others call out stereotypes associated with the description. The game sparks discussion about the power of prejudice. Jacob remembers speaking of how, when he briefly had to use a wheelchair after a car accident, he faced the stereotypes met every day by the disabled.

"I was blown away by the emotional impact," Jacob says of his first retreat. He began working to expand the program. In his junior year, he brought more than 150 students from 15 local high schools together for a March 1996 convention on unity and tolerance. The theme—"Together Again"—was based on "Pangea," the theory that all the continents were once a single land mass.

"I thought it would be great if all the schools going their separate ways could come together to resolve the conflicts that surrounded us," he says. "If we could look back at Pangea, we could learn a lot about ourselves and our present situation."

A second convention Jacob helped organize in April 1997 attracted about 100 more students. But for Jacob, now a freshman at the University of California at Berkeley, "the neatest aspect was that the conventions were planned for students, by students. The organizers were determined and committed—the most powerful students on campus."

jacob green

OCTOBER 10, 1997, LOS ALAMITOS, CALIF.

Bill

Bill and Christina Verigan took a family vacation to Cambodia and Vietnam in the summer of 1995. What they saw—countless adults and children who had lost their limbs to landmines—shocked them.

"I saw so many people in Phnom Penh [in Cambodia] without limbs begging in the streets in rickety wheelchairs and on makeshift crutches," Christina says.

When they returned home to Wyckoff, N.J., Christina, 16, and Bill, 13, began working with the International Campaign to Ban Landmines (ICBL) to promote the Ottawa Treaty, an international agreement banning the use of land-mines. President Clinton has not signed the treaty, claiming that the United States needs mines to protect troops patrolling South Korea's tense border with North Korea.

"Without the treaty, we have nothing," Bill says, "because even though mines are being removed, there are more being planted."

"It makes me wonder: Whose side are we on?" Christina says.

Along with supporting the treaty, Bill says, "You must help the innocent civilian victims who require rehabilitation, artificial limbs, financial support and plain love."

Bill says public awareness is the key to the U.S. campaign. "Americans don't understand what it's like when every step you take could be your last."

Bill has written a newsletter and sent it to government leaders. The siblings have designed anti-mine posters, which have been exhibited internationally, spoken at rallies in Washington, D.C., and met with 1997 Nobel Peace Prize winner Jody Williams, ICBL's leader. And they've challenged their peers to get involved.

"Write letters. Convince legislators. Get supporters to sign petitions," Bill tells the student groups he speaks to about the campaign. "Don't worry about being politically correct. Be morally correct."

DECEMBER 8, 1997, WYCKOFF, N.J.

bill verigan

AND

christina verigan

Bill and Christina Verigan with the mine weapon they want to ban.

photograph by brian velechenko

Most

people don't spend a lot of time thinking about their sewage system. But residents of Southwick, Mass., are glad Kassia Randzio, 16, did. Back in sixth grade, she and some friends studied the town's waste-removal system as part of a school project. What they learned was so alarming that they started a campaign to build a new sewer system.

Southwick's current system, Kassia says, "is basically a cement box, with sand underneath to filter leakage. A truck comes around to carry the sewage to another town's system."

The problem is that when sewage leaks out of the septic tank, it could seep through the sand and contaminate the public's drinking water. That's the part that grossed out Kassia and her friends. They helped organize a public forum on the issue, and Kassia later spoke before 400 neighbors at a town meeting. She was persuasive: Residents voted to build a new system.

That was four years ago. Today, the preliminary work has been completed, and construction of the $8.3 million sewer system should begin this spring.

"Because kids were doing the work, I think adults listened more than they would to other adults. They viewed us as being innocent and honest," Kassia says. "We had no hidden agenda like politicians might have."

Kassia has remained involved with the project and is working to improve it. For example, the town acquired out-of-use railroad beds under which it will lay the new sewer lines. Kassia proposes to turn this strip of land—now used illegally as a dumping site—into a scenic trail for biking, hiking and in-line skating.

Kassia lobbied at the state capitol in Boston for passage of a bill to set aside state funds for projects like her "rails to trails" proposal. The bill passed, and now Kassia is working with town leaders to apply for funding for Southwick.

Kassia, a sophomore at Southwick-Tolland Regional High School, hopes the trail will be complete by the time she goes to college. "I won't be able to use it, but at least it will be there for others to enjoy," she says.

Kassia's work for Southwick helped make her a runner-up in the 1997 **react** Take Action awards, for which she won the right to distribute $25,000 worth of clothing and merchandise to local children's charities.

"I don't think teens realize that what they think or say can make a difference," she says. "Hopefully, people will look at me and say, 'If she can do it, why can't I?'"

JANUARY 19, 1998, SOUTHWICK, MASS.

kassia randzio

The

letters come from girls who are frustrated, who lack support from their family, friends and teachers. They want to succeed in math and science and excel in sports, but they can't.

Mavis Gruver, 17, of Duluth, Minn., has been reading the letters since she, her twin sister, Nia, and her mother started New Moon magazine in 1993. By girls and for girls, with 20 girl editors between the ages of 8 and 14 and as many as 100,000 readers around the world, New Moon challenges stereotypes about what girls can and can't do and offers them support.

"Girls know what girls care about, what they are concerned about," Mavis says.

Mavis does more than just produce the magazine. She also speaks out for young women. She has been an active participant at international conferences, including the State of the World Forum held in San Francisco last fall, where she spoke both on media images of youth and women's leadership.

This summer, Mavis worked on the 150th anniversary of the Women's Rights Convention, the first of which was held in 1848 in Seneca Falls, N.Y., and celebrated in that town last month. At that first convention, women discussed their lack of educational and employment opportunities and pressed for the right to vote, which women did not receive until 1920.

As part of the Girls International Forum, a worldwide action group she helped found, Mavis worked to update the historic Declaration of Sentiments written at the first convention. In the update, called the Girls' Declaration of Sentiments, Mavis and her friends raised modern issues such as the media's treatment of girls, sexual harassment and the inequality between girls' and boys' sports. "It stated our hopes and dreams for the future," she says.

"We've come a long way, but have further to go," Mavis says. "The world needs to listen to young women today, because they will be the leaders of tomorrow. Many are savvy and extremely well informed, but we need to get them involved in making decisions that affect their future."

AUGUST 17, 1998, DULUTH, MINN.

mavis gruver

53

photograph by michael bowles

"I think I'd feel a complete sense of hopelessness if I lived in a country where I could not talk freely," says Rachael Tanker, a senior at Richard Montgomery High School in Rockville, Md. "I'm trying to fight that hopelessness."

Rachael, 17, is co-president of her school's Amnesty International chapter, which works to raise awareness and support for people around the world who have been jailed, tortured or killed by government authorities for speaking up about their political or religious beliefs.

Last February, Rachael and other Amnesty International members drew chalk outlines of nine bodies on the sidewalk leading up to their school's entrance. The drawings represented the Ogoni 9, a group of nine Nigerian citizens who demonstrated in 1995 for a more democratic form of government in their African country. The nine were charged with causing the murders of four government officials who were killed when the demonstration turned violent. The group was later jailed and executed, despite worldwide protests.

"We wanted people to see all this injustice and get involved," Rachael says. "We had a lot of people come up and ask questions about what was going on."

Rachael and her group also passed out fact sheets on the Nigerian government's rights abuses and asked fellow students to sign petitions requesting that President Clinton and Secretary of State Madeline Albright pressure Nigeria to respect human rights.

In addition to raising awareness about Nigeria at her school, Rachael participated in a larger demonstration in Washington, D.C. Outside the Nigerian Embassy, she and others rallied to rename a nearby street corner after the leader of the Ogoni 9, Ken Saro-Wiwa.

Their efforts to rename the street were unsuccessful, but Rachael says she plans to keep working for human rights: "I want to do something to stop people from being killed unjustly in the future. If I were put in jail for an unjust reason, I would want help getting out. Everyone deserves a fair trial and fair punishment."

DECEMBER 7, 1998, ROCKVILLE, MD.

rachael tanker

When

she was younger, Liberty Franklin would come home after school to a dark apartment and find her alcoholic mother sobbing. She never met her father and lost her only picture of him. Her older brothers were in and out of jail, and her older sister was a drug addict.

Liberty, now 17, grew up with a lot of pain. But she didn't let it bring her down. "I weighed things out," she says. "I decided I wanted a better future for myself."

How did she pursue this? In sixth grade, when her friends began drinking, Liberty began going to the local Boys & Girls Club for help with her homework. There, she says, "the staff members took me under their wing. At the club, I was able to get away from the drug peddling and violent gangs on the street and the negative things in my family."

At the club, she tutored children and helped organize events like Breakfast With Santa and a back-to-school clothing drive. She also joined a leadership group for girls, where they talked about things "like peer pressure and family life," Liberty says.

She gained confidence, enough to speak honestly to her mother and persuade her to stop drinking. "Now she's in her third year of sobriety," Liberty says proudly.

Liberty also began taking more responsibility at home. To help out financially, she worked as a bank teller and fast-food cashier even as she kept up with her schoolwork.

Now a senior at Everett (Wash.) High School, she's ranked as one of the top students in her class. This spring she will be the first one in her family to graduate from high school.

For her leadership and academic efforts, in September Liberty was named The Boys & Girls Clubs' National Youth of the Year and was given a $10,000 scholarship.

As the representative of 3 million club members, she has met President Clinton and will travel around the country to discuss important youth issues with business and government leaders.

Liberty says her goal is to help boys and girls overcome obstacles such as poverty, crime and family problems.

"All I've done is to avoid the cycles of negativity. Little did I know I was leading my life by example," she says. "Now I'm proving to my peers that they can do it, too."

liberty franklin

DECEMBER 14, 1998, EVERETT, WASH.

photograph by zee wendell

When

Lauren "Lo" Detrich was just 3 months old, doctors told her parents that she would be lucky if she saw her 20th birthday. Lo was born with cystic fibrosis, a fatal lung and digestive disease.

But Lo, now 14, is a fighter. To control her illness, she takes 50 pills every day, and for three hours each day she uses two special machines that help her breathe. "Every breath of life is a prayer answered," Lo says.

Though medical treatment for cystic fibrosis has gotten better since she was a baby, and Lo now can expect to live to at least age 30, she is doing whatever she can to raise money to find a cure.

She has worked for the Cystic Fibrosis Foundation's Great Strides walk-a-thon since the fourth grade, when she collected $600. "My goal has been to make more money each year than the year before," says Lo, who was the nation's top fund-raiser for the walk-a-thon last year, bringing in nearly $50,000.

Lo was able to do this with the help of a family friend who promised to match up to $20,000 of the donations Lo collected. So Lo persuaded hundreds of friends and businesses in the community to contribute to the walk-a-thon. To raise even more, she and her friends also held a dance and a bake sale.

Because of her great success at raising money, Lo's cystic fibrosis chapter named her chairperson of the walk-a-thon, a position usually held by an adult. In that role, Lo asks local businesses and schools to donate money and participate in the 6-mile walk.

Lo, an eighth-grader at Monte Cassino Middle School in Tulsa, Okla., also is the spokesperson for her chapter and talks to the media about the need for more research.

"I believe I'm going to get better," she says, "but I can't do it without help. Every minute you give to helping someone with cystic fibrosis is like giving a minute of life back to that person."

MAY 3, 1999, TULSA, OKLA.

lauren detrich

photograph by doug hoke

photograph by julie bidwell

Don't

even think of messing with 19-year-old Christine Sargent. For the past four years, she's been studying—and teaching—ways that girls and women can defend themselves. "If you're assaulted," Christine says, "there are five major targets to go for: the eyes, nose, throat, groin and knees."

Christine isn't trying to be tough, just safe. When she was a freshman at Taos High School in New Mexico, she learned that rape and domestic violence were on the rise in her hometown. Instead of living in fear, Christine felt women should take steps to protect themselves. She helped raise money to fly in women's defense instructors from Los Angeles and co-founded the Taos Women's Self-Defense Project.

Since then, Christine has honed her survival skills and helped train 20 new teachers who hold free workshops.

The most challenging thing Christine has done, she says, is teaching self-defense classes to high school girls. "It was hard because they were trying to act cool," Christine says. "But even in that age group, a lot of people had already dealt with sexual harassment, like going to parties and having drunk guys hitting on them."

The best thing women can do in a scary situation is take an active role in protecting themselves, Christine says. "We focus on three things: making sure a woman is aware of her surroundings, being assertive and self-defense."

The physical part is simple, she says. A combination of kicks and punches directed against weak points is the main idea.

"I want other young women to feel as empowered as I do. It feels great to have these skills to rely on," Christine says.

Christine recently received Hitachi's Yoshiyama Award for community service. In the fall, she'll attend Scripps College, an all-women's school in California—where, we're guessing, the student body will soon be safer than ever.

JULY 15, 1996, TAOS, N.M.

christine sargent

"**The** factory is noisy, filled with dust. Workers aren't allowed to talk. There is constant pressure to produce. If you don't complete your production quota, you must stay until you do—without pay."

For Abby Krasner, 16, of Brattleboro, Vt., the list of abusive conditions at overseas factories where children make sneakers, clothes and soccer balls for American consumers is familiar. Now Abby wants to make those conditions known to all Americans—and get them to do something about changing them.

Abby has spoken out at events throughout Vermont. She and her classmates at Brattleboro Union High have sent dozens of letters to newspapers and companies like Nike and Guess. And she worked with U.S. Rep. Bernie Sanders last fall to get Congress to pass a law that bans the import of products made with forced child labor.

The National Labor Committee (NLC), a consumer watchdog group, estimates that the labor cost for a pair of Nike shoes made in China, Indonesia or Vietnam is about $2.60, yet the shoes sell for an average of $80. "Not enough people know about this," Abby says. "The more I learned, the more passionately I became involved."

A Nike spokesman confirmed the estimated labor cost of the shoes. However, he says, "The retail price doesn't include overhead, materials and factory profit." Nike recently announced that it would end child labor and improve conditions at its factories. "It is a good first step," Abby says. "However, they did not change their wages, which means adults still won't make enough to support their families."

Workers at factories that make Nike shoes in China, the NLC estimates, may earn as little as 16 cents per hour for 12-hour shifts. "Kids in these situations aren't necessarily better off if they're not allowed to work—they need to help their families. Children will be forced to find other jobs so their families can be fed," Abby says. "But I hope other corporations will look at Nike and start to change."

"Young people need to make our voices heard, because we are the number one consumers of products made by children," Abby says.

JUNE 15, 1998, BRATTLEBORO, VT.

abby krasner

When he tell his friends what

they can find in cigarettes, they "freak out a little," says
Michael Higgins, 13. "They learn that they're inhaling
formaldehyde, something scientists use to preserve human
bodies."

Michael, of Monroeville, N.J., is doing everything he can to
persuade people to stop smoking. For starters, he's responsible
for his community's ban on cigarette vending machines—an
idea that has quickly spread to five nearby communities.

Michael wanted vending machines to be banned because, he
says, they're an easy way for kids to buy cigarettes. Michael's
mother got hooked at a young age, and he wants to keep others
from developing lifelong addictions.

"My mom has tried to quit smoking three times," he says.
"I saw my friends smoking in the fifth grade, and I was
concerned that they would get addicted like my mom."

Michael has been an anti-smoking activist since he was 11,
when he joined the Municipal Alliance, a community group that
educates people on the dangers of drugs, alcohol and tobacco.
Through the group, Michael has learned to teach his peers about
the risks of cigarette smoking.

But wanting to do more, Michael decided to take legal
action. So he came up with a simple solution: Get rid of the
vending machines.

Michael wrote up his idea and presented it to local government
officials. Several meetings were scheduled to discuss the
proposal, and Michael attended each one. The final vote was
unanimous.

Has the ban stopped teens from smoking? There are no official
statistics, but Michael says he has personal evidence: "Two of
my three friends who smoke have quit. I'm working on the
third."

Now an eighth-grader at Upper Pittsgrove School, Michael
was honored as Youth Advocate of the Year by the Campaign for
Tobacco-Free Kids in Washington, D.C., last April. He was
given a $1,000 scholarship and met with President Clinton in
the Oval Office.

Michael continues to do anti-smoking work. He gives talks to
students at local schools and is working on a puppet show to
teach younger kids about the dangers of smoking. "You have to
get to the kids," Michael says. "Even the tobacco industry
knows that. But I hope to get to them first."

michael higgins

MARCH 22, 1999, MONROEVILLE, N.J.

photograph by david moser

Karen

Chan of Oakland, Calif., cut classes, drank, did drugs and hung around with friends who were in gangs. Just two years later, she changed her life completely, by passing out more than $5 million to youth programs that give kids something better to do.

Karen, now 18, says she was motivated to make a difference after watching a TV news report of a shooting in San Francisco. "People in my neighborhood were getting shot all the time, and the news media didn't care because we were people of color and poor. It made me angry," she says.

So Karen fired off a letter to a columnist at her local paper expressing her outrage. He noticed the well-written letter and recommended Karen to Children's Express, a national news service written by young people.

Karen was assigned to interview a young girl "who was exactly like me. I realized that I couldn't do what I was doing anymore," she says. "It was really scary to see what I had become."

Karen decided to change her life. She avoided her old friends and wrote more stories for Children's Express, even covering the 1996 Republican National Convention in San Diego.

That year, Karen also got involved with Kids First, a program set up by Oakland to create youth programs. Karen was one of nine young people selected along with 10 adults to decide where $5 million would go. It was one of the first times ever that kids participated in the way a U.S. city would spend its money on youth.

"It was very stressful," Karen says. "But it was also a good feeling knowing that the people trusted us."

After 18 months, Karen and the rest of the committee voted on 40 projects, ranging from a youth chorus to cultural enrichment programs. "We felt good knowing that there would be more alternatives for kids than getting involved in gangs," Karen says. "We wanted them to have things to do that they were interested in. We wanted them to take responsibility for making their lives better."

The reaction from youth in Oakland has been positive, Karen says, adding that Kids First could have made a difference in her life. "If I had seen people involved in something productive, I would have gotten involved too," she says.

Now a freshman at Mills College, Karen was awarded a scholarship from the National Foundation for Women Legislators for her community service, and she continues to find time to volunteer.

Karen wants kids to know that they too can turn their lives around and make a difference. "You learn different things from everybody," she says, "so think about who you choose to hang out with now. It may affect you in the long term."

APRIL 5, 1999, OAKLAND, CALIF.

karen chan

photograph by darcy padilla

The parties that teens went to in Milwaukee, Wis., three years ago worried Toni Martin. "There was a lot of bad stuff happening," the 17-year-old says, including shootings, alcohol and drugs.

Toni knew there were better ways to hang out. She had heard about Safe Night—a program that gives teens safe places to party without drugs or alcohol—and decided to check it out. She had such a good time, she says, that she decided to help organize more overnight parties at her local community center.

"There is music and lots of dancing and lots of food. And there's basketball and pool," Toni says. The Safe Night parties, held every other month, begin at 8 on a Friday or Saturday night and last until 8 the following morning. No alcohol, drugs or guns are allowed, and the 200 young partygoers are supervised by adults.

"You don't have to carry a gun to feel protected," Toni says, "and you don't have to get high to have fun."

Toni also provides some of the entertainment at Safe Night parties. Her group, Mixed Generation, sings inspirational songs and directs role-playing skits about solving conflicts in nonviolent ways.

"A lot of people fight just because they don't want to look like a punk in front of everybody else," says Toni, a junior at Madison University High School. "We tell them to walk away if someone gets in their face or to talk it out. It's all about being strong-minded."

Safe Night parties started in Milwaukee in 1994 and have since caught on across the country. On June 5, thousands of communities will join in the first national Safe Night USA, a project of Wisconsin Public Television. The event will be broadcast live on PBS and BET and will feature a performance by Mixed Generation.

Toni hopes it will be an annual event. "It helps people realize that they can solve problems in a nonviolent way. And it's a lot of fun."

MAY 31, 1999, MILWAUKEE, WIS.

toni martin

When

international activists got together to discuss nuclear weapons, war crimes, pollution and other problems at the 1998 State of the World Forum, they didn't just hear from politicians, businesspeople and scientists. Thanks to Megan Klein, 18, of Park Forest, Ill., they also listened to the voices of young people.

"When you look at global population, youths are almost 50 percent," says Megan, who helped to bring five dozen young activists from lands as varied as Nigeria, Bosnia, Northern Ireland and Ecuador to the international conference. "If you're going to talk about global issues, issues that affect everything—issues that affect youth—how can you do it without talking to youth?"

Megan, who began working at a drop-in center for teens in suburban Chicago when she was 15, first attended the State of the World Forum as a youth delegate in 1997. She thought the event was an amazing way for activists of all stripes to meet and share ideas, but she also felt that young people's opinions were ignored. Young delegates were allowed to attend meetings but not to appear as speakers; the adults got hotel rooms, while the young people went to youth hostels.

"Most of the youths shared the same feeling of not knowing why they were there," she says. "They hadn't felt respected." Instead of complaining, Megan led her fellow activists in devising a plan to put young leaders on panels and roundtables right alongside the adults (and to get young delegates real hotel rooms). And after graduating from high school last year, she moved to San Francisco to work as an intern for the forum—to make sure her ideas were being carried out. They were.

In October, the 60 young activists who came to the forum from around the world were recognized as full-fledged participants. Megan says she was most affected by young people who were living through war and its aftermath in Bosnia, Cambodia and Nigeria.

"Listening to them tell their stories—and their work to make sure other people don't have to go through what they went through—was just heartbreaking," Megan says. "Everybody came away with a new outlook on the world they're living in—and how you can change it."

Megan herself is already working on that. Postponing college for a year, she'll go to Washington, D.C., in the spring to work for the nonprofit National Network for Youth. Then she'll head to Northern Ireland to help plan the 1999 State of the World Forum. And come summer, she'll travel to Tanzania for three weeks to work on improving life in rural villages there.

"Once I started getting involved with youth empowerment," Megan explains, "it just lit a fire in me."

megan klein

JANUARY 11, 1999, PARK FOREST, ILL.

photograph by black/toby

The photographs showed children from Third World countries who were born with cleft lips and cleft palates. The gaps in their lips or the roofs of their mouths made it difficult for them to smile or laugh.

"I saw the pictures four years ago, and they really affected me," says Courtney Smiles, 17, of Lawrenceville, N.J. She learned that these children have trouble talking and eating and that many of them are hidden away in shame by their parents and don't go to school. Courtney wanted to do something to help. She joined Operation Smile, an international network that raises money to provide free reconstructive facial surgery for children and young adults. Last fall, Courtney traveled to Santa Domingo, Ecuador, joining 35 medical volunteers, her club adviser and one other teen.

"It was just incredible," says Courtney, whose responsibility was to bring comfort to the 3- to 8-year-old patients before and after surgery. "Many of them hadn't ever seen Americans, let alone doctors with face masks and scrubs. They were frightened," she says. Courtney talked to the children with the help of two teen Ecuadoran translators and played with them with the toys she and her group had brought. "We were the children's safe haven," she says.

During her 10-day stay, Courtney also traveled to local day-care centers and orphanages to teach children about nutrition and dental hygiene and passed out free toothpaste and toothbrushes. "The people were so friendly, so thankful for simple things," she says. "I learned to find happiness in simpler things, like someone's smile." Now a senior at Lawrence High, Courtney is the president of her school's 140-member Operation Smile club, which last year raised $8,000 for 11 surgeries worldwide. She also speaks at other schools to encourage students to start clubs. "We can change kids' lives completely," she says.

NOVEMBER 2, 1998, LAWRENCEVILLE, N.J.

courtney smiles

73

Fernando

Pantojas, 17, lives in a tough Chicago neighborhood. "Gangs and drugs are so predominant that some have come to accept them as normal. I've learned that's not true," he says. "Now I try to help younger kids understand. I hope I can get through to them in a way that gang members and drug pushers can't."

Fernando's base of operations is the General Robert E. Wood Boys & Girls Club of Chicago. He spends five hours a day, five days a week there. To encourage kids to hang out in a safe place, he organizes games of basketball and hockey as well as computer and library sessions. Fernando wants kids to stop joining gangs and to stay away from activities and company that lead to trouble.

A senior honors student at John F. Kennedy High School, Fernando says he avoided trouble himself because his family places a lot of hope in his future. "I try to be a positive influence," he says. "Gang members really don't want to be in gangs, and they need help in getting out…they need someone to talk to."

Fernando organizes his activities, including a community cleanup day and holiday food drives for the homeless and hungry, to build confidence in the kids so they won't have to turn to a gang for recognition.

"One person can't save everyone…but I think I've helped some get through," he says.

JUNE 10, 1996, CHICAGO, ILL.

fernando pantojas

Kristen Deaton, left, created the Anyone Can Softball League for young people with disabilities.

photograph by doug hoke

As a softball star in Oklahoma City, Kristen Deaton, 18, experienced all the highs and lows of competition. But the special-needs children with whom she volunteered never got to experience that excitement.

"There was something missing in their lives," she says. "There weren't many recreational opportunities where they could enjoy each other and meet new friends."

Two years ago, Kristen filled that need by launching the Anyone Can Softball League for young people with disabilities. "My mom and I talked about creating a team for a while," Kristen says, and, when she was 16, "we decided to stop talking about it and do it." Her mother, a physical therapist who works with children with disabilities, helped Kristen come up with the format for league games: a modified version of softball in which most players use a batting tee and volunteer "buddies" help do whatever a player can't.

In 1995, the Deatons invited nearly 300 local children with special needs to join their fall league. "By February," Kristen says, "we had more than 70 players and four teams, and plenty of volunteer buddies."

A local community-service group loaned its softball fields to Anyone Can and altered the park's entrances, dugouts, bathrooms and concession stand to make them accessible to people with disabilities. During the league's second season, more than 100 children played on six teams. "We seemed to get a new player every week," Kristen says.

Now a freshman scholarship softball player at the University of Tulsa, Kristen has already started a league in that city. She says she also plans to start Anyone Can leagues for bowling, basketball and even soccer.

"Everyone says we've done a lot of hard work, but we don't see it that way," Kristen says. "All we've done is give these children an opportunity to have something all their own. It's their uniform. It's their team. And their parents now have the chance to watch them play and feel their joy. I'd work a hundred times harder just to see their smiles."

For her work with Anyone Can, Kristen was named one of 10 national runners-up in the **react** Take Action Awards program last year, earning the honor of donating $25,000 worth of merchandise to local children's charities.

kristen deaton

OCTOBER 6, 1997, OKLAHOMA CITY, OKLA.

When
16-year-old Molly Browne from Shorewood, Wis., was in eighth grade, she and a friend participated in the 10-kilometer Walk for AIDS along Milwaukee's lakefront.

During the walk, they stopped at an information booth for Camp Heartland, a summer camp for children from across the United States who either have HIV or have lost a parent or sibling to AIDS. The girls ordered Heartland t-shirts, which arrived along with information on volunteering for the camp. Molly started volunteering in its Milwaukee office once a week. When Molly met some Heartland campers, she quickly became convinced that she needed to help more kids experience the fun of summer camp.

"It was devastating for me to see these children who were dying. Being with them solidified my desire to help," she says. Molly threw herself into raising money for the 5-year-old camp. Bake sales and t-shirt sales raised about $400. A magic show she helped organize as president of Shorewood High School's Students Against Social Apathy club helped, too. But she thought she could raise more with a big event: a benefit concert.

"I had no idea where to begin," she says, so she started asking for help. The Globe, a popular Milwaukee nightclub, donated space for the concert; local funk and ska bands volunteered to perform; and Molly's friends and classmates covered the city with 2,000 fliers hyping the event. The work paid off. Molly's first concert for Heartland, on April 13, 1996, raised $1,200. A second show, last Dec. 9, raised another $1,200. More than 250 teens filled the Globe for each show, and Molly plans to put on a third concert later this year.

When Molly turns 18, she will be able to volunteer as a counselor at Heartland, which runs weeklong sleep-over camps for as many as 350 children in different cities each summer. Until then, she plans to continue volunteering to spend time with children with AIDS or HIV. "No matter how many times I listen to them speak, I'm always so struck by their strength and courage," she says. "If I can help them, I will. Any way I possibly can."

molly browne

SEPTEMBER 8, 1997, SHOREWOOD, WIS.

Molly Browne with Camp Heartland campers Bruce, left, and Anthony, who have lost family members to AIDS.

photograph by black/toby

TWO teens with a keen awareness of the environment are the founders and operators of a nonprofit corporation with a mission: planting trees in their city.

The duo—Tara Church, 18, and Sabrina Alimahomed, 17, both of El Segundo, Calif.—are known as Tree Musketeers. They began their careers as environmental activists back when they were both 8. The two young activists planted their first tree, a budding sycamore they named Marcie the Marvelous, to give something back to the Earth. Planting Marcie was so empowering for them, Sabrina says, "that we couldn't stop there."

The two went on to form the band of Tree Musketeers, which branched out with a bushel of projects. Nine years later, that group is still going strong. Tree Musketeers is now a nonprofit corporation run by youths, for youths, with its own office in El Segundo. Sabrina, now a freshman at local El Camino College, manages a Tree Musketeers project to improve their hometown. The work has included planting additional trees in the area known as Memory Row, where Marcie was first planted. Joining Marcie now is a whole street lined with trees, each with a plaque dedicating it to a loved one or the celebration of a birth, marriage or anniversary.

A senior at El Segundo High School, Tara is working on her Tree Musketeers project called Partners for the Planet. Started two years ago, it's a series of national and regional summits where teens can share ideas on what can be done to aid environmental efforts. The Partners project also includes a magazine, Grass Roots Youth, circulated to 50,000 teens all over the world.

"I'm so proud of the work we've done with Partners," Tara says, "mostly because it is so far-reaching." The Musketeers' newest project is called Tree House, which Sabrina says is an outdoor community classroom. "We leased a property in town that was an eyesore, and we're cleaning it up, planting trees and turning it into an area where young people can come learn about the environment," Sabrina says.

When the two girls get "too old" for the Tree Musketeers, they "will hand over the reins" to younger people, Tara says. "My wish," she adds, "is to make other teens see that every single one of them is extremely important and extremely powerful in their ability to effect change. It all starts with just one individual's determination to make a difference."

tara church

A N D

sabrina alimahomed

MARCH 18, 1996, EL SEGUNDO, CALIF.

Sabrina Alimahomed, left, and Tara Church founded Tree Musketeers, a nonprofit corporation to plant trees in their community.

When

Rashad Williams heard about the shooting at Columbine High School in Littleton, Colo., "I was devastated," says the sophomore at San Francisco's Archbishop Riordan High School. But the case of Columbine student Lance Kirklin had an especially powerful effect on Rashad.

Lance had been seriously wounded, suffering injuries to his chest, face, knee, foot and thigh, and had no medical insurance to pay for the surgeries that would allow him to walk again. "I'm a runner," says Rashad, 15, who has been into track since he was 8. "When I heard about Lance, I wondered what I would do if that happened to me."

Rashad decided to use his athletic ability to help Lance. He signed up for San Francisco's annual Bay to Breakers race, then asked people to pledge as much as they could. "Bay to Breakers is a big event," Rashad says. "It was the only way I could think of to raise money quickly."

Speed mattered—the race was only a week away. Fortunately, Rashad's mission became a local news story, and money started pouring in: He raised $12,000 before he even hit the road.

The tough part? Rashad had no time to train. The Bay to Breakers course is 7.5 miles, far longer than the 400- and 800-meter races Rashad usually runs for his school's track team. "I had cramps and wanted to stop, but I just kept thinking about Lance," he says.

Rashad didn't cross the finish line first, but he says he feels like a winner because he has raised $40,000 to help Lance. "Being able to help made me feel really good inside," Rashad says.

Lance, who's now walking, may ultimately face $1 million in medical bills, and he's thankful for Rashad's help. "He's a great young man with a big heart. It means a lot to me that he did this for a complete stranger."

Lance and Rashad are no longer strangers. They've met a few times and exchange e-mail often, forging a friendship that will definitely go the distance.

SEPTEMBER 6, 1999, SAN FRANCISCO, CALIF.

rashad williams

Rashad Williams, right, raised money to help Lance Kirklin, a victim of the Columbine tragedy, pay his medical bills.

photograph by brian kelsen

*Whoever dreamed up
'me first' when describing this
generation hasn't met these teens,
whose compassion for others
comes a long way before themselves.
Their hearts are leading their actions
and inspiring others to follow.*

compassion

Joey Russell, left, with his best friend, Kate Shelley, and her mother, Mary. Joey sold a piece of history to help Mary pay for a lifesaving surgery.

A TITANIC GIFT

Well before *Titanic* the movie, Joey Russell, 13, was fascinated by Titanic the story.

At an antiques show four years ago, he discovered a Titanic postcard, which had been printed soon after the ill-fated ocean liner sank in 1912. He bought it for $100. Two years later he and his grandfather took a cruise to the site where the ship sank to watch an attempt to raise it to the surface. The attempt failed. But on the cruise, Joey met Titanic survivor Edith Haisman, then 99, who signed his antique postcard. Haisman has since died. But the postcard she signed may now help save a life.

Mary Shelley, the mother of Joey's close friend, Kate, 14, recently learned she had leukemia. Mrs. Shelley was told that a bone marrow transplant could save her life. But she needed help to raise the $80,000 required, after insurance coverage, to pay for the procedure. So neighbors in Havre de Grace, Md., and friends at the Jacob Tome Institute, where Joey and Kate will be ninth-graders this fall, began raising funds to help.

Joey offered to auction off his Titanic postcard. "I knew I had something really valuable," he says, "especially with the craze over the movie." Joey hoped the card might bring in $1,000 or even $2,000.

But then a neighbor contacted *The Rosie O'Donnell Show* about Joey's auction plans. O'Donnell, who was 10 when she lost her mother to cancer, invited Joey, Kate and Mrs. Shelley to appear on her show. And on April 16, as Joey talked to O'Donnell on TV about the auction, the cast of the Broadway musical *Titanic* burst onto the stage, singing a song from the show they had rewritten in Joey's honor. The cast then handed Joey an oversized, $60,000 check for his postcard, which is now displayed in the lobby of the musical's New York City theater.

The check from the show's producers, combined with the $20,000 neighbors had already raised, gave Mrs. Shelley enough money to pay for her operation. She is now undergoing treatment at a Seattle hospital.

"When I found out Joey was auctioning off the postcard, I was really surprised," Kate says.

"I feel like anyone would do what I did if they had the chance to save someone's life," Joey says.

JUNE 22, 1998, HAVRE DE GRACE, MD.

joey russell

Rick Weismiller and Emily Interlandi must be ready to ride at a moment's notice.

photograph by suzanne mapes

He usually drives an old Volkswagen Beetle. But when Rick Weismiller is on call as an emergency medical technician and his pager beeps with news of an auto accident or other emergency call, he bolts out of class and takes the wheel of an ambulance.

"Driving an ambulance is a lot different than a Beetle. It's hard, but not that tough once you get the feel for how long and wide it is," says Rick, 18, a senior at Darien High School in Connecticut. Rick is one of 55 Darien student volunteers at Explorer Post 53—a state-certified all-teen emergency medical team that has responded to local emergencies for 28 years.

"When I started, I didn't realize what a commitment it is," says post president Emily Interlandi, 18. Training starts freshman year, when teens put in 40 hours learning to monitor police scanners. As sophomores, trainees ride along in one of the post's three ambulances, learning to assist the fully trained EMTs. Next comes a 120-hour course in EMT procedures. After that, if a volunteer has turned 16, he or she can become a certified EMT and driver with the responsibility of getting a crew to an emergency as quickly as possible.

"I've sure learned how to deal with situations under a lot of stress," Emily says, "especially when you get calls during the middle of the night and haven't had much sleep."

Two 24-hour shifts are required of volunteers each month, but most work more often. A shift begins at 5:30 p.m. The crew spends the night on bunk beds at headquarters and in the morning takes its ambulance to Darien High, where members wear a pager in case of a call during the school day. The crew is always accompanied by an adult EMT.

Emergency calls require quick thinking and creativity. Emily responded to one in which a construction worker had fallen from a ladder and sustained massive head injuries. "To get him to the ambulance," she says, "we had to make a bridge over the house's foundation. It was pretty tricky."

Rick has been called to a number of grisly auto accidents on Interstate 95, which runs through Darien. "I've been at several drunken-driving accidents," he says. "I don't let my friends do it because I've seen what happens."

MAY 4, 1998, DARIEN, CONN.

rich weismiller

AND

emily interlandi

When Aimee Furber climbed

Mount Kilimanjaro, Africa's highest mountain, she didn't do it to set a record, although that's what ended up happening. She did it to help raise money for others who are struggling to climb their own "mountains."

Her goal was to raise money for Committed Partners for Youth, a program that pairs at-risk teens with trained adults in Portland, Ore., Aimee's hometown. The adults provide guidance and support for teens who are at risk of dropping out of school, becoming involved in gangs or drugs or similar problems.

"Climbing a mountain doesn't seem nearly as hard as the climb out of rough circumstances that many young people face," Aimee, 13, says. "We did it to give more young people a chance to improve their lives."

Aimee trained for the climb for one year by going hiking and taking folk dancing, which helped develop her breathing capacity and endurance. In January, Aimee, her parents and 16 other adults made the trek to Tanzania in eastern Africa. Only seven people in the group actually reached the 19,340-foot summit, with Aimee becoming the youngest American ever to make it to the top.

"The difficulty was dealing with the altitude," she says. "You get dizzy and nauseous because of the lack of oxygen."

With stops at night to eat and sleep, it took the climbers four days to reach the top. "I just took one step at a time," Aimee says.

Each hiker was able to come up with about 100 friends and sponsors who would commit themselves to helping the Climb for Kids. So far, $41,000 has come in. It will be used to train the mentors for eighth-graders at three Portland schools.

"It's really cool that I'm able to help others by going, and not just go for myself," says Aimee, who is already set to tackle the mountain again.

AUGUST 10, 1998, PORTLAND, ORE.

aimee furber

photograph by reid horn

91

After

you've run 500 miles in your athletic shoes, chances are you're ready for a new pair. But what to do with the old ones? Philip Hamer, 16, of Trabuco Canyon, Calif., gives old shoes new life by donating them to people who have none.

A junior at El Toro High School, Philip started collecting shoes when he was 6 with the help of his dad, a marathon runner. They distributed fliers at races, asking runners to donate shoes they no longer wore. Word spread quickly through magazine and newspaper articles, and over the past 10 years, Philip and his family have collected and distributed more than 150,000 pairs.

"It's been a total family effort," Philip says. His mom, sister Erica, 13, and brother Patrick, 10, pitch in. They pick up, unpack and sort the shoes, then deliver them to places that help the homeless.

Through mission groups associated with their church, Philip and his family have sent shoes to needy people in countries as far away as Russia, Nigeria and Burma. However, most of the shoes they collect are given to shelters in Southern California.

"Right here in Los Angeles are people who go barefoot, too," Philip says. "When you see what a huge deal it is for someone to get a pair of shoes, it makes you think about all we have and all we take for granted."

Last December, the Hamers held a "shoe party" with about 20 friends in an effort to get 2,000 pairs of footwear sorted and disinfected. Most of the donations were athletic shoes, Philip says, but they also received some genuinely weird stuff. "Somebody donated a pair of blue suede shoes in memory of Elvis," Philip says. "But the best are those that are durable and comfortable."

Recently, Philip and his father took shoes to a shelter in Venice Beach. "It was totally cool to meet the people who started this house to help the homeless," Philip says. "It showed me that one person could really make a difference. Get involved—you can change hundreds of lives."

philip hamer

MARCH 8, 1999, TRABUCO CANYON, CALIF.

photograph by stewart volland

As a TV reporter delivered the news last spring, Grace Sanders got nervous. A tornado packing 160 mph winds was whipping through her city of Nashville, Tenn.

"Suddenly the TV went out and the room went black," says Grace, who was at a beauty salon having her hair cut. She ducked for cover under a table as the tornado roared by. "I could hear stuff hitting the roof and things falling against the building," she says.

After a few minutes, it was over. "The whole side of the building across the street had crumbled," she says. "But it was when I saw all the trees bent halfway down to the ground that I got really scared." Later Grace learned that the tornado had wiped out more than 20,000 trees. "It was amazing," she says. "I didn't think anything like that could happen in Nashville."

Last November, Grace got the chance to help replace some of those trees. She asked 12 friends to bring old clothes and a shovel to her 16th birthday party. But instead of sitting down to birthday cake, Grace and her friends joined up with other volunteers from ReLeaf Nashville, a nonprofit group. The teens planted nine trees just a few blocks from the hair salon where Grace had seen the tornado.

"It was hard work, but we really got into it," says Grace, a sophomore at Hume-Fogg High School. The volunteers had to pull out the roots of the dead trees and dig deep holes. It took a team of three to hoist up each new tree for planting into a new dirt home.

But Grace says the effort was worth it because the residents in the neighborhood were so grateful. "It gave us a good, warm, fuzzy feeling inside," she says. "And it was fun. It wasn't your normal birthday party."

APRIL 19, 1999, NASHVILLE, TENN.

grace sanders

To 14-year-old Angela Hedian, the bloody civil war in the African nation of Rwanda seemed remote. That all changed when one orphaned child's voice traveled thousands of miles and set Angela in motion.

Two years ago, Angela's eighth-grade teacher at St. Mary's School in Rockville, Md., read a letter from a young woman named Cathy Burke, who was working as a missionary in Rwanda. Burke described the conditions in Rwanda, where thousands of children have been orphaned. Then she described how one 8-year-old boy in an orphanage she visited asked for her shoes. Burke couldn't give him the shoes because she didn't have a spare pair. But she did send the message in her letter back to the United States.

The letter made Angela realize how much she took for granted. Then it got her thinking about what she could do to help. "I knew I couldn't change the world," Angela says, "but I could take some steps to make a few people's lives better."

With the help of her principal, Angela began to collect shoes. She placed bins at the entrance to the school and asked students to donate footwear. After a few months, Angela had over 500 pairs of shoes, more than enough for each child in the orphanage.

Now came the toughest part—getting the shoes to Africa. Angela contacted several airlines, trying to persuade them to deliver the shoes. One airline employee refused, saying, "Africans don't wear shoes."

"When I heard that, I sort of had a hissy fit," Angela says. "They don't wear shoes because they're too poor to have them."

Finally, a Rwandan airline agreed to transport the shoes. After they arrived, Cathy Burke wrote and reported how happy the shoes made the Rwandan orphans. "Cathy said that as she was passing out the shoes, she could actually see the children's faces lighting up," Angela says. "She said it was like Christmas."

The shoe drive was so successful that Angela repeated it as a Girl Scout project. This fall, Angela will enter 10th grade at the Academy of the Holy Cross, where she'll continue to put her best foot forward.

AUGUST 19, 1996, ROCKVILLE, MD.

angela hedian

When

people say Molly Vandewater's house is a zoo, they don't mean it as an insult. Walk through Molly's garage and you'll find it lined with cages, not cars. At any given moment, her parents' bathroom can take on double duty as an incubator for newborn hummingbirds. Even the baby pool in her backyard has a unique purpose—it's used to house water-dependent birds. The reason for all the remodeling? Molly, 16, runs a hospital for wounded animals, and she is doctor, nurse and janitor all in one.

It all started when Molly was 12 and living in Arizona. She volunteered to work with a wildlife rehabilitator and learned how to nurse injured animals back to health. When her family moved to Thousand Oaks, Calif., she found that the rehabilitation center there wasn't big enough. So Molly and a handful of others formed Wildlife Care of Ventura County— and decided to make Molly's house the main hospital.

Molly has made sure her home is equipped for the task. It houses 32 birdcages, five incubators, 18 cages for other animals and five outdoor aviaries. "We've never turned anyone away," says Molly, who gets her patients from animal-control officials, veterinarians and the public.

At first, it was hard not to get emotionally attached to her patients, but as the volume grew, Molly had no choice but to let go. Would she keep any as pets? "No," she says firmly, explaining that wild animals should be returned to nature, where they belong. "It's neat to see a bird whose life you've saved be released."

Molly, who gets up at 5 a.m. to study, also volunteers at a local pet emergency clinic. "Giving animals a second chance at life is a special feeling," she says. And she doesn't plan to cut down her hours any time soon; she's in pursuit of another goal—becoming a veterinarian.

DECEMBER 2, 1996, THOUSAND OAKS, CALIF.

molly Vandewater

In the remote parts of the states that make up Appalachia, many people have to get by without electricity, plumbing—sometimes even outhouses. Amy Downing, 19, knew how the people there lived from her older brother, David, who volunteered with his church youth group to repair homes in the summer. "Many live in houses their great-great-grandfathers built with their bare hands," she says.

Amy, of Richardson, Texas, was eager to help. Like her brother, she hooked up with the Appalachia Service Project, a nonprofit group that sends volunteers to rural Kentucky, West Virginia, Virginia and Tennessee. She first learned basic construction skills and then joined a team of six others to work on homes badly in need of repair.

During her first summer with the program, Amy, then 16, spent a week insulating a garage that would later be used as a home. The new house did not include plumbing, however, because there wasn't enough money to complete the job. "When I got home," she says, "I promised I would never turn on my faucet again and not be thankful."

Amy says the experience was eye-opening and that she has learned much from the people she has helped. "The people who live there have a special relationship to each other and the land," she says. "They have a better sense of what's important in life. Family is everything to them."

"I love my family," she adds, "but after this experience I know I take them for granted."

A freshman at the Music Conservatory at the University of Cincinnati, Amy has worked in Appalachia the last three summers and plans to return again this summer. "It's a trade-off," she says. "We give them the material things they need, and we get the spiritual things we're lacking."

JUNE 7, 1999, RICHARDSON, TEXAS

amy downing

Patrick

Monahan helps the homeless every Christmas. Using his allowance and other earnings, he fills a sack with chew toys, catnip, honey and nuts. Then, like Santa, he heads out to visit the less fortunate—unwanted animals at a shelter near his home.

"It's a good feeling to brighten an animal's day," says Patrick, 14. "They've been in cages all day, so to make them happy for a couple of moments is worth it."

Patrick's love of animals began when he was 5 and his mom took him to a shelter near their home in Moreno Valley, Calif. Patrick remembers feeling bad for the animals in cages. And at age 10, he began volunteering at the shelter.

Since then, Patrick has organized everything from adoption promotions to dog washes. ("Looking fluffy makes you more adoptable," he says.) He has even starred in *Pet Time*, a local cable-TV show.

Because of his concern for animals, Patrick last year was selected as a finalist in the American Humane Association's Be Kind to Animals Contest. The recognition was "neat," he says, "but the important thing is to get more people to volunteer at shelters. When you help out, other people help out."

Patrick recently moved to Chester, Conn., with his parents and dogs, Scruffy, Asia and Manny. He was sorry to leave his friends at the Moreno Valley shelter, but "it's nice to have started something and know the animals will be continuously cared for," he says, "maybe even spoiled."

And anyway, Patrick, a freshman at Valley Regional High School, has already found new friends at a nearby shelter. "I'm glad to play their Santa," he says.

FEBRUARY 1, 1999, CHESTER, CONN.

patrick monahan

In the fourth grade, Elienne Lawson was determined to be a professional singer. She loved to sing, and she had the special gift of perfect pitch—the ability to hit every note perfectly, every time.

Then, at age 9, Elienne's dream collapsed. Struck with a disease called viral encephalitis, she lay in a coma for three weeks, close to death. When she woke up, she couldn't see or hear.

But she was alive—and for Elienne, that was enough.

She regained her sight, but her hearing didn't return. "Elienne realized very quickly what her deafness meant," her father, Greg, recalls. "She said to me, 'I can't sing if I can't hear.' It didn't take her long to accept her fate."

But Elienne refused to let go of music. She asked her parents if she could take piano lessons. And without being able to hear a single note, Elienne, now 16, has become an accomplished classical pianist. Even her music teacher doesn't understand how she does it.

In Elienne's silent world, the sense of touch has taken over where hearing left off. "Sound is a function of vibration," she explains. "When someone sits next to me, I can feel their heart beat. Music for me is a swelling of vibration throughout my whole body. My body is one big ear. When you're swimming in the ocean, currents move you in and out—they ebb and flow. That's what music is like for me, calming and soothing."

elienne lawson

Elienne hopes one day to play for deaf children. For now, she volunteers her time using sign language to read to them. With the help of her father, she invented a device that removes moisture from hearing aids. It has proved to be so useful that Elienne is now president of her own successful business. "I'm at the best time of my life now," she says. "I want to learn all about everything."

Elienne, a senior at Moorestown High School in New Jersey, plans to go to college next fall with the help of a scholarship from the Discover Card Youth Program.

"Courage," Elienne says, "is not what you do on the battlefield or emergency room, but in the quiet moments when no one is watching. I'm most proud of the fact that I never cried, never felt bad about being deaf. I just accepted it. I have taken my greatest obstacle and made it my greatest achievement."

SEPTEMBER 16, 1996, MOORESTOWN, N.J.

photograph by david moser

photograph by reid horn

Sean

Sean Redden was never himself when he entered "Glenshadow's Tavern," his favorite online chat room on the Internet. On the afternoon of April 14, the 12-year-old from Denton, Texas, was the character "Meegosh," a medieval dwarf from the 1988 movie *Willow*. Sean stuck to his character as he chatted with other sorcerers, heroes and villains, some friends of his, some strangers from around the world, all connected by their computers. But then something happened that made Sean stop playacting.

Someone using the screen name "Susan Hicks" typed "Help me." Another user responded, "I am the healer of the tavern…poof, you're healed."

But "Susan" wasn't acting. "I can't breathe," she continued. Sean, who suffers from asthma, identified with her problem. "Are you really sick?" he asked. "Do you really need help?"

"I assure you this is no hoax," she typed. The woman told Sean she was Taija Laitinen, a 20-year-old business school student in Kerava, Finland, near Helsinki, where it was 2 a.m. She had been working late in a computer lab at school but suddenly was having trouble breathing, and her legs had gone numb. She couldn't get out of the room to find a phone, so she went on the Internet and stumbled into Sean's chat room.

When Sean saw her messages, he called his mother over, and they phoned their local sheriff, who began a chain of international calls that led to a Finnish emergency rescue team.

Meanwhile, Sean stayed online with Taija, asking her about her location. He relayed her answers to his mother, who was on the phone with a police operator, who was on the phone with an operator in Finland.

"It was all very exciting," Sean says, "but very frustrating, too. It took forever to get messages back and forth."

Sean had been online with Taija for 90 minutes when she typed, "I hear them, but they've run past me!"

"Hold on, they'll get to you, don't worry," Sean responded.

And then, finally, Sean read, "They're here! Thanks. Bye."

A couple of weeks later, Finnish police notified the Denton sheriff's office that Taija had been rescued and treated at a local hospital. In July, she called Sean to thank him and let him know she was feeling better.

"My whole family has asthma," Sean says. "I was thinking if this were them, they would need help. Most people would have helped like I did."

sean redden

AUGUST 11, 1997, DENTON, TEXAS

Lauren

Garsten, 19, knows a good match when she sees one. She should: She has spent most of her spare time over the last few years pairing up needy kids with elderly companions who didn't feel needed.

The idea came three years ago when Lauren was working at a home for abused children. "I was thinking about senior citizens who don't feel important anymore," recalls Lauren. "Getting them together with kids who desperately wanted someone to care about them made perfect sense."

Lauren, of Cheshire, Conn., entered her idea in the Wesleyan (University) Challenge, a program that recognizes teens who want to make the world a better place. She won $2,000 to pursue her matchmaking plans.

Lauren recruited other students in her school, who served as go-betweens for the kids and the seniors. "The purpose was just to have fun, to provide a good time for a few hours one Saturday a month," explains Lauren. "We went to the petting zoo, museums, apple picking, things like that."

It took some time to get over the shyness, but most outings ended with the children opening up to their older friends. "The children were so unused to being around people they could trust," says Lauren. "It was great to see them with people they could count on."

Now a freshman at Harvard University, Lauren says she learned a lot from the people she met. "I found that no matter how different you are from someone, you can always find a common link—something to talk about."

"It was hard to say goodbye when the program ended," says Lauren. "But the smile I got the last day from the shiest kid in the group told me we had made a difference."

lauren garsten

JANUARY 13, 1997, CHESHIRE, CONN.

photograph by julie bidwell

When

Qun Hui Chen came to the United States four years ago from Fuxing Province, China, she barely knew any English. But that didn't stop her from becoming a volunteer at New York Downtown Hospital, where she used her skills to help others and make friends in her new country.

Every day after school, Qun Hui, 17, pitched in at the hospital, logging in an astonishing 480 hours in one year. At first, her friends couldn't understand why she'd want to spend so much time working for no money. "C'mon, get a real job," they'd nag. But mastering office procedures, feeling needed and, most important, fitting in in America meant more to Qun Hui than earning a paycheck. "I wanted to meet new people and have a chance to learn," she says. And, since half of the hospital's patients are Chinese, she also served as a translator.

Qun Hui's dedication paid off. Last June, she was named Top Volunteer of the Year by New York City Mayor Rudolph Giuliani. She was presented with her award at an elaborate ceremony at City Hall. "I felt famous! It was such an honor to meet the mayor," remembers Qun Hui, who is an honor student at Seward Park High School in New York.

Doris Lederman, Qun Hui's supervisor at the hospital, wasn't surprised that her favorite helper was given an award. "Qun Hui is an excellent, energetic person" with a good work ethic, she says.

Although Qun Hui's parents want her to go back to their homeland one day, she admits that readjusting to life in China would be difficult. "The U.S. is not as male-oriented as China," says Qun Hui. "The democratic system, educational opportunities and freedoms make America very special. I've adopted this society," she says. "I like it here."

JANUARY 20, 1997, NEW YORK, N.Y.

qun hui chen

Richard Jones, right, entertains
a friend at the V.A. hospital.

Unlike
most 18-year-olds, Richard Jones spends a lot of his free time hanging out with men in their 80s and 90s.

Richard built his bridge across the generation gap at the Veterans Affairs Medical Center in Washington, D.C., where he has been a volunteer for the last three years. "I looked for a place where I could spend as much time as I could helping people," Richard says. Since 1994, he has put in more than 1,300 hours with sick and aging veterans at the long-term care unit. Sometimes that means talking, sometimes playing checkers, sometimes simply listening.

Out of dozens of war stories Richard has listened to over the years, one from a 97-year-old man who was imprisoned by the Germans during World War I stands out. "He told me how his legs were shot off as he was held hostage," Richard says. "I didn't blink once when he was speaking and almost cried listening to what he went through—it was live history for me."

Another ex-soldier, Richard says, was stricken with Alzheimer's disease, which impairs the memory. "He kept calling me Billy. He'd say, 'Billy, get in the car,' as we were being seated in the dining room at the hospital." When Richard reminded the vet that they were at a table, the man shot back: "This is my fantasy. Let me finish."

Compassion didn't always come easily for Richard. "I didn't used to have respect for elders, or self-confidence or motivation," he admits. "Through these years at the V.A., I've gained it all. Now if anyone needs me, I am right there. It's made me a better person." His efforts have also brought him awards from the Daughters of the American Revolution, the National Caring Foundation and the Horatio Alger Association.

Although befriending people who are ill and dying can be painful, Richard says it has helped him deal with one of the most difficult parts of life. "Death is hard," he says, "but I've learned how to handle it, and I know they are going to a better place. I help keep their memories alive."

FEBRUARY 17, 1997, WASHINGTON, D.C.

richard jones

photograph by julie bidwell

The residents of the Mercy Shelter in Hartford, Conn., last fall shared a 3-ton vegetable donation from an unusual source: the garden of Brandon Mulcunry, 14, of nearby Farmington. Brandon grew the food for the homeless shelter and soup kitchen as a project to earn his Eagle Scout rank. "It didn't take a green thumb," he says, "but it took a lot of time."

The City of Farmington rents 50-by-50-foot garden plots to residents for $25 apiece. Brandon leased two plots and then convinced local seed companies to donate a variety of vegetable seeds to the project. His fellow Scouts and their families—100 people in all—also helped by donating their time on a regular schedule to keep the garden growing.

Brandon began planting in May 1996, sowing the garden with peppers, eggplant, turnips, beets, green beans, two types of tomatoes, three kinds of squash and a variety of herbs. When summer arrived, Brandon spent up to three hours a day in the garden, harvesting crops and trying to keep the bugs away—without using chemical pesticides. "We had a lot of bugs in the eggplant. I think they were potato beetles," he says. "They were so annoying. We would go down a row picking them off the plants and crushing them on the ground, and then we'd turn back around and there would be even more."

By the end of the growing season last October, Brandon had devoted more than 1,000 hours to the project. The people who run Mercy Shelter, which survives on a tight $39,000 yearly food budget, were glad he did. And Brandon says making the donation made him feel good, too. "The people living there were just ordinary, really nice folks," he says, "not at all like the stereotype of those you might think live in shelters."

This summer Brandon and his family have headed back to the garden. They are contributing their time to another Scout growing project, as well as tending two plots of their own. The food from the garden will be donated to Mercy Shelter and a Hartford battered women's shelter.

"We knew that they needed help, and we decided to help them," Brandon says. "It would be nice if everyone helped a little bit. The size of the garden doesn't matter. Every little bit helps."

AUGUST 25, 1997, FARMINGTON, CONN.

brandon mulcunry

The

trick looks easy. Magician Kevin Kaplowitz puts a bottle into a silver paper bag, then turns the bag upside down while keeping one hand on the bottle through the bag. "They always think they've got it figured out," Kevin says, "but then I crumple up the bag, and the bottle truly disappears, and they're amazed."

Like any good magician, Kevin, 16, won't reveal the secret of how he makes the bottle disappear. But it's no secret how much joy he brings to the children who make up his favorite audience.

Kevin, a junior at Sonora High School in La Habra, Calif., has been performing magic since he was 4. He started his career with his older sister, Karen, a dancer, actress and clown. The siblings entertained regularly at local hospitals, bringing cheer into patients' lives.

Today, Kevin puts on shows for children at the Shriners Hospital for burn victims, the Children's Hospital of Orange County, the Orangewood Home for children and at local Boys & Girls Clubs. His act mixes mind-blowing illusions with a touch of humor.

"My sister and I still perform together whenever we can, although she's at college now and working at Disneyland, so it doesn't give her as much time," Kevin explains. Or as he tells his audiences, "She's studying to be a doctor and likes to perform open-wallet surgery."

Kevin's commitment to helping others goes well beyond pulling rabbits out of hats. He donates to local children's charities all the money he earns from performances at restaurants, corporate events and private parties. He hasn't kept track, but he knows his donations have run into the thousands of dollars.

Kevin hopes one day to attend medical school and become a pediatrician, but he says he'll always find time for magic. "The most important thing is believing in yourself and trying to make a better tomorrow for everyone," he says. "The reward is in the smiles that appear."

NOVEMBER 24, 1997, LA HABRA, CALIF.

kevin kaplowitz

photograph by tim hale

For his Eagle Scout project, Richie Hiatt, 14, of Los Alamitos, Calif., decided to raise money to help families of children with cancer. He thought he could raise $500 or maybe even $1,000 at best. But when he later learned that his own 7-year-old sister was diagnosed with leukemia, his ambitions for the project grew.

"I saw Laci suffer through the chemotherapy," Richie says. "I saw her throw up, and I saw her hair fall out." Motivated by his sister's struggle, he spent seven months planning his fund-raiser, Walk On for a Cure for Cancer. Richie wanted it to take place at Los Alamitos High School, where he will be a freshman this fall. He made the walk short—a quarter-mile around the school track—because his sister wanted to walk the entire distance herself, despite the pain it would cause her. "If my sister couldn't walk the whole walk, I would carry her," Richie says.

Richie received support from his Boy Scout troop, church, school and business groups. Newspapers and TV stations publicized the event throughout the Los Angeles area.

Then, on a spring day last year, more than 200 people arrived at the high school track. As the theme from *Rocky* played, Richie led the walk with Laci, who had been in the hospital with a fever only the day before. Two cancer patients joined them, and other teens with cancer showed up to lend their encouragement as well.

The walk took only 10 minutes, but it generated donations for almost a year. Richie's walk eventually raised almost $16,000.

Richie sent the money to Parents Against Cancer, a nonprofit organization in Long Beach, Calif., which helps kids with cancer whose parents have limited financial resources. The money is being used for costly medications, checkups, transportation to hospitals or clinics, refrigerators to store medicines—even wigs for teens who have lost their hair.

"If you believe in yourself and your cause, others will too," Richie says. And Laci, now 8, is doing fine. Her cancer is in remission.

AUGUST 3, 1998, LOS ALAMITOS, CALIF.

richie hiatt

photograph by tim hale

Ballet

was her life. And Brooke Lyons expected it to be a big part of her future. But all that changed in the summer of 1995. Brooke's parents had traveled from their home in Woodbridge, Conn., to visit Brooke at the Boston Ballet's summer dance program. "My muscles were aching from dancing," says Brooke, now 17. "They treated me to a massage at their hotel."

But as the masseuse rubbed Brooke's back, she said casually, "Oh, you have scoliosis, don't you?"

"There I was, lying on the table, saying, 'scoli-what?' " Brooke says.

Brooke did, in fact, have scoliosis—an abnormal and sometimes painful curvature of the spine. Her doctor told her to wear a back brace 18 hours a day to help limit the curving of her spine until she reached her mature height. She only took it off to dance.

While the brace supported her spine, Brooke says, she needed emotional support as well. But when the National Scoliosis Association told her that its closest chapter was two hours away, Brooke started a Connecticut chapter herself. Today, that chapter has more than 100 members from age 9 to 80, and Brooke is its president. Along with organizing monthly meetings, Brooke talks to school nurses to stress the importance of early scoliosis screenings.

And last December, she organized a benefit performance of *The Nutcracker* with her ballet company, the New England Ballet. Brooke danced the lead role and raised $10,000.

After the show, she found out that the Scoliosis Association had named her its national teen spokeswoman.

Brooke, a junior at The Hopkins School in New Haven, Conn., will soon have surgery to straighten her spine. A year later, she'll find out if she can dance again. But she says she has other goals now, like helping teens deal with scoliosis: "Teenagers have issues they need to discuss with someone their age. Parents or doctors can't relate to concerns such as what your friends at school think when you wear a brace, or how it affects your social life."

JUNE 8, 1998, WOODBRIDGE, CONN.

photograph by garth dowling

The

Snake River, Idaho's largest, was rising to a dangerously high level, threatening to flood farms and homes. A record snowfall from the previous winter was melting, feeding the problem. It was the highest the river had risen in more than 70 years. So Craig Whyte got to work.

Beginning Memorial Day weekend in May, 1997, Craig, along with thousands of others, started sandbagging the river's banks, trying to prevent a flood. He worked 10 to 12 hours a day for 21 days straight.

"We spent all our time trying to keep ahead of the constantly rising river," says the 18-year-old native of Blackfoot, Idaho. "Wherever you were needed, that's where you went, whether it was to fill bags with sand or get up to your knees in mud putting the bags at the river's edge. Sometimes, we'd have chain gangs up to a mile long passing the bags."

The sandbag wall that Craig helped build was 8 feet high, 6 feet deep and nearly a mile long. But it couldn't hold back the river forever. Eventually the river rose so high and became so powerful that it raged through the wall, devastating nearby property. "Fifty homes in our school district were three to five feet underwater for nearly a month," he says.

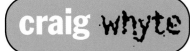

Craig rallied students from area high schools to help clean up some of the homes. "We ripped out carpet, scraped mud out of basements, moved furniture, stripped walls, painted—whatever was necessary to get the homes ready for their families," he says.

While cleaning up the homes, Craig noticed the frightened children. They had been sleeping in nearby schools or in their families' garages. They couldn't play outside because there was too much water and mud. "I realized," Craig says, "that children were the forgotten victims of the flood."

Raising money from local businesses, Craig led the effort to create a day of fun activities for the young flood victims. He called it Day Away.

On July 10, 50 children came with their families in rowboats, tractors and four-wheel drive vehicles to the local high school for a day of free bowling, games, prizes and even "I Survived the Flood of '97" t-shirts.

"When a lot of people work together for the same cause, they can change lives," says Craig, who is a freshman at Utah State University and a winner of the 1998 Prudential Spirit of Community Award. "I know. I saw it happen."

SEPTEMBER 7, 1998, BLACKFOOT, IDAHO

The playground can be a dangerous place.

More than 70,000 kids nationwide were injured last year in swing-set accidents, according to the Consumer Product Safety Commission. As a result, some towns had started taking swings out of their parks. So four Nevada teens decided to do something about it.

"We thought the number of injuries was pretty scary," says Lyndsey Franks, 14.

"All of us remembered falling off a swing when we were little," says Derek Smoot, also 14. "We really wanted to do something to make our parks safer."

While students at Hyde Park Middle School in Las Vegas, Derek and Lyndsey, along with Lindsey Bean, 14, and Ashley Berg, 15, designed what they call the "back belt," a safety strap that can be clamped onto swings and adjusted for size. "When you lean back on a swing," Lindsey says, "it keeps you from falling."

The four first sketched their ideas, then built a model. After testing it on kids ages 3 to 14, they made some adjustments.

Last April, the four young inventors were named finalists for the Bayer/National Science Foundation Award for Community Innovation. The competition asks teens to solve serious community problems that may be overlooked by adults.

In June, the four students were flown to Orlando, Fla., to meet the established inventors who judge the contest. At the end of the week, they learned they had won the first prize—a $5,000 U.S. savings bond for each of them.

"It's an elegant, simple solution to a significant problem," contest judge Art Fry, who invented the Post-it note, said of the back belt.

The teens, now ninth-graders, have applied for a patent and are negotiating with a toy manufacturer. They hope to sign a contract this month and go into production soon. Two Las Vegas elementary schools already have expressed interest in purchasing the belt.

"Swing sets were being removed in our community to prevent injuries," Lindsey says, "but we found a better way to protect kids and still let them enjoy the fun of swings."

SEPTEMBER 28, 1998, LAS VEGAS, NEV.

lyndsey franks

derek smoot

lindsey bean

AND

ashley berg

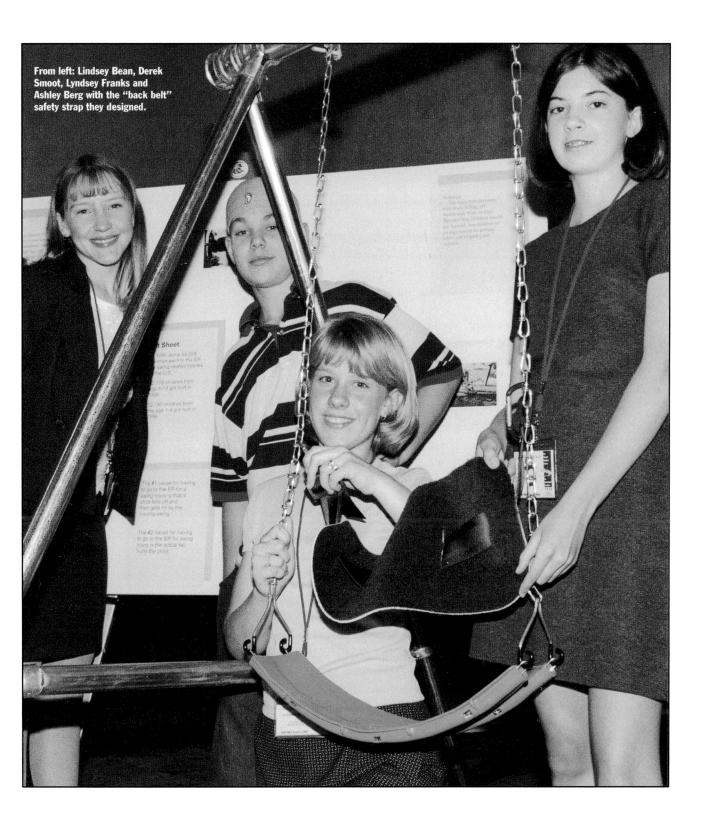

From left: Lindsey Bean, Derek Smoot, Lyndsey Franks and Ashley Berg with the "back belt" safety strap they designed.

Cacie

Cacie McHugh was a newspaper carrier making her usual rounds three years ago when she happened to learn that one of her customers, a woman in her late 80s, hadn't eaten for three days. "The woman was kind of casual about it," Cacie says. "She said she just had forgotten to eat."

Cacie, now 18, realized there were probably other people in her small hometown of Verden, Okla., southwest of Oklahoma City, who needed help.

"Many of the people on my paper route were in their 70s and 80s," Cacie says. "They didn't have family around, and they were living alone. Some weren't physically able to take care of themselves."

Concerned, Cacie contacted meal-delivery programs in neighboring towns, but "they were over their limit already," she says.

With the help of her youth pastor, friends, family and the owner of Vivian's Cafe, a local diner, Cacie developed Nutrition Mission, a program in which several homebound senior citizens could receive the cafe's lunch special of the day for whatever they could afford to pay. Cacie personally delivered the hot meals to the people at their homes each day during the summer. Her pastor helped during the school year.

Cacie and her friends, who helped support the project with bake sales, soon realized that the senior citizens needed more than the meals. "Lots more wanted to be in the program," she says. "And they were hungry for friends, too."

So Cacie decided to start a nutrition center where the elderly could eat with their friends. She wrote letters to her state senator and representative, who helped provide state funding, and she got permission from local leaders to use the town hall's dining room for her center.

But, Cacie says, "The building wasn't in the best shape. We had to do a lot of painting and cleaning and fixing up. Luckily, plenty of people volunteered to help."

In January 1997, the Verden Senior Nutrition Center opened. Today, 25 senior citizens enjoy hot, nutritious meals there five days a week. They also gather there to play cards and bingo.

Cacie, now a freshman at the University of Central Oklahoma in Edmond, won a $5,000 award this year for her community service from The Hitachi Foundation.

She continues to visit her friends at the center but remains concerned about those who are not there. "There's always somebody in need, and they are often overlooked. We need to look for them and help them out."

cacie mchugh

NOVEMBER 23, 1998, VERDEN, OKLA.

photograph by doug hoke

The effect of nuclear radiation and what it does to children is constantly on Megan Doherty's mind. The sophomore from Mount Assisi Academy in Lemont, Ill., first heard about the problem when a speaker came to her school and told her class about a nuclear reactor accident that occurred 13 years ago in Chernobyl, Ukraine.

"She told us the effect of the explosion was a hundred times greater than the Hiroshima bomb during World War II," Megan says.

Megan learned that the explosion, which occurred when she was just a baby—April 26, 1986—still affects the people who live in Chernobyl. "There is still so much radiation around in the air, the water supply and the soil," she says.

Megan knew she had to do something for the children of Chernobyl, who must cope with problems such as cancer caused by radiation fallout. So she decided to work with Camps for Children of Chernobyl, a nonprofit group that places children in U.S. summer camps.

But Megan needed to raise money to bring the kids, ages 9 to 15, to this country. So she asked local groups for money and volunteers.

After six months, she raised $20,000—enough for 13 children and their doctor to attend a camp last summer in Lake Geneva, Wis., for three weeks and to spend two more weeks with families in Megan's hometown.

"They liked swimming the best," Megan says. "They can't swim where they live because of the radiation."

Megan, 15, says she's looking forward to seeing some of the same people again this summer. She has raised $12,000 toward that goal. "We don't believe how fortunate we are until we understand what others don't have," she says.

APRIL 26, 1999, LEMONT, ILL.

megan doherty

This

summer, Michael Johnson, a 6-foot-2-inch, 195-pound defensive end on his football team, is taking a week off from his usual training schedule. Instead of sprinting and lifting 250-pound weights, he'll be lifting the spirits of young people who have muscular dystrophy.

Michael, 17, a junior at John Carroll Catholic High School in Birmingham, Ala., knows something about muscular dystrophy. Last summer he worked with kids who have the often life-threatening genetic disorder that causes the muscles to weaken and waste away. Michael's football coach asked him to join him in volunteering at a muscular dystrophy camp about 80 miles from Birmingham, one of 85 such camps around the country. "My coach has an 8-year-old nephew who has the disease," Michael says, "and he told me working at the camp would be a life-changing experience."

Michael wondered if he was up to the challenge. But the camp staff told Michael and the other volunteers that all they needed for the job was compassion. "The counselor told us that some of the young people come to the camp kind of down, and that just by bringing a smile and a good attitude to the situation, you could make their day," he says.

More than half of the 42 campers, age 6 to 21, were in wheelchairs, and all were paired with a volunteer. Michael spent a week paired with Stephen Lingo, 18, who is in the later stages of the disease.

The two shared a room along with five other campers and five other counselors. Michael helped Stephen brush his teeth, wash and dress, as well as participate in such activities as canoeing and swimming.

At first, swimming wasn't easy. "It was his first time in two years," Michael says, "and he was afraid of the water. But I told him to rely on me. And it helped him relax." With Michael's help, Stephen ended up staying in the water for two hours. "He didn't want to come out," Michael says. "He was having too much fun."

Though Michael gave much of himself, he found he got much more in return from the friends he made at camp. "You're supposed to be there to make their day, but they end up making yours," he says. "It was a blessed event for me to experience the everyday life of these kids. Able-bodied people take for granted something simple like walking. But now I feel fortunate that I can walk, let alone play football."

Stephen, who reports that "it was fantastic" having Michael as a counselor, is doing well now and hopes to return to the camp this summer. Michael looks forward to seeing him again and also looks forward to helping other campers. "Doing service is good not just for the community," says Michael, "but for your soul."

michael johnson

MAY 24, 1999, BIRMINGHAM, ALA.

Michael Johnson with camper Stephen Lingo.

Allison Gold, left, and Bojana Radivojevic share an international friendship.

photograph by david moser

Life in Bosnia had become a nightmare for Bojana Radivojevic (boy-ANA radee-VOYE-vich) and her younger brother, Gordan, as a brutal civil war tore their nation apart. "We stayed in our basement for months in fear of having our home bombed," Bojana says. "For many there was no food, no electricity, no water, no education. Religious persecution, war camps and living in fear of being killed were a part of our lives. It was amazingly terrible." Bojana says that 58 of the 60 children in her sixth-grade class died or were injured in the war.

But Bojana and Gordan were lucky. They were among a group of students brought to the United States by the American Friends Service Committee for the 1994-95 school year. Bojana, then 14, became a sophomore at private Abington Friends School in Jenkintown, Pa., where she made a new friend, Allison Gold of Langhorne, Pa.

Later, when Allison heard Bojana and Gordan would not be able to return to Abington for the next school year because there wasn't enough money, she decided to raise the funds herself. "Someone had to do something to bring Bojana back," says Allison, now 18 and a freshman at Penn State University.

Allison wrote an emotional letter to Abington parents and graduates, telling them what Bojana and Gordan had given her and her classmates: "These two students turned our lives around. They made us realize that every place is not a happy one," she wrote. "They taught us to treasure the things life brings us—our families, our school, our friends, our houses, our food and most of all, our opportunities."

Abington families contributed enough money to keep Bojana at the school for her junior and senior years. Bojana, now 18, is a freshman this fall at Elizabethtown College in Pennsylvania. She returns to Bosnia each summer to visit her parents. After spending seventh and eighth grades at Abington, Gordan returned to Bosnia, where a peace treaty has been signed.

Bojana and Allison have spoken to several school groups about their experiences, urging teens to get involved when they see people in need. "Study and be aware of situations," Bojana says, "and do what you can to help the children."

allison gold

SEPTEMBER 29, 1997, LANGHORNE, PA.

The top three fund-raisers and their teacher: Jeff Hunt, Marc Brinson, Mrs. Mills and Brandon Wood (l-r).

Marc

Brinson had been looking forward to taking Sandy Mills' science class last fall. He had heard that she was one of the best teachers at Traverse City (Mich.) West Junior High School.

"She loves to teach," says Marc, an eighth-grader, "and kids can feel her enthusiasm."

But Mrs. Mills had to leave after the second week of school. She learned that she had breast cancer, and she needed to begin her treatment quickly.

Chemotherapy, radiation and surgery all weighed heavily on the teacher's mind—and on her finances. She wasn't sure how she would manage.

Marc and other students wanted to help. So they began working on a bowling party fund-raiser, where members of the community could donate or pledge money for each pin knocked down. Forty-five teachers and local police officers volunteered to bowl.

The students went door to door in their neighborhoods after school and on weekends asking for pledges. In a few weeks' time, money started rolling in. "It wasn't hard," Marc, 13, says. "Most people in my neighborhood know me and donated."

Marc raised the most money of anyone else in his school, more than $600. "I just wanted Mrs. Mills to return," he says.

Brandon Wood, 14, agrees. "We wanted her to know that people actually care."

In addition to the bowling party, students raised money by selling postcards designed by an art teacher and by promoting an auction of Beanie Babies and gift certificates to local restaurants and inns.

Just before Thanksgiving, teachers asked Mrs. Mills, who was recuperating from surgery, to visit the school, where they presented her with a surprise—a check for more than $11,000. When she got on the public-address system to thank the 1,500 students, cheers and applause erupted throughout the school.

"I was totally blown away," says Mrs. Mills, who will use the money to pay for her growing expenses.

Students are looking forward to their teacher's return this month. "We didn't just raise money for her," Brandon says. "We also helped raise her spirits. And I'd do it again in a heartbeat."

APRIL 12, 1999, TRAVERSE CITY, MICH.

marc brinson

Rachael

Nadeau isn't much different from other teens in Bristol, Conn. She plays volleyball and runs track in high school. She hangs with her boyfriend and her friends on weekends. And for five years, she has delivered the afternoon paper to 56 homes in her neighborhood. But last winter, the 15-year-old carrier for the Bristol Press made a mark on one woman's life that won't be forgotten for a long time.

A few years earlier, Rachael had struck up a friendship with an elderly woman on her route. The two started talking when Rachael stopped by one weekend to collect. Rachael would shovel her driveway and buy groceries for her after snowstorms. Often they would get together for a game of Scrabble. "She's 92 years old," Rachael says, "but she's really cool."

Then one day in February, Rachael noticed that the woman hadn't brought in her newspaper in three days. Rachael knocked on the door and got no answer. Instead of finishing her route, she went to her own home nearby and telephoned her customer. Once again, no answer. So she returned with her mother. "I knocked and looked in every window," Rachael says, "and through the very last window, I saw what I thought was a blanket or sheet on the floor. And then I saw a foot move."

Rachael ran to call 911. When the police arrived, they found the frail woman alive but suffering from a broken shoulder. Two nights earlier, as she was trying to get into bed, she fell on the floor and couldn't stand up again. She had been there ever since. She was overjoyed to see Rachael. "Every time I need her, she's there. She's my best friend," says the woman, who prefers to remain anonymous.

For her rescue effort, Rachael was honored at the state capitol and received a special citation from the Connecticut General Assembly.

"Before the incident, every week I was sure to go in and say hi," Rachael says. "Now I go to see her every day. It's not an obligation—it's something I want to do."

OCTOBER 21, 1996, BRISTOL, CONN.

rachael nadeau

Sixteen-year-old

Ta-Keesha White knows all about the tough times. She never got to know her father. And her mother suffers from a disease that makes it difficult to leave home, let alone work. So, for most of her life in Springfield, Mass., Ta-Keesha and her family have just scraped by.

But last year, Ta-Keesha's luck began to change. She won a scholarship to the prestigious Northfield Mount Hermon boarding school in Northfield, Mass. And now she's poised to become the first person in her family ever to go to college.

While most people would be content to chill out and enjoy the good times, Ta-Keesha says, "Since I have a full scholarship, I feel like I have to give something back." So she volunteered for her school's Big Sisters program.

Since last September, she's spent about two to three hours a week with 10-year-old Heidi Cyr, a fourth-grader at Northfield Elementary. Ta-Keesha says she knows how important it is to be a positive role model. Sometimes that just means hanging out with Heidi. At other times, it means being there to listen when Heidi needs her.

Heidi is living with her grandparents while her parents are sorting through family problems. "Sometimes Heidi needs to vent out all her problems and talk for hours," Ta-Keesha says. "I listen and let her know I've been through the same kind of problems—that I'm 16 and I've never had a conversation with my father. And I try to keep her feeling good about herself and tell her things will get better."

Has Heidi changed since becoming Ta-Keesha's little sis? "Yes! She's changed a lot," Ta-Keesha says. "She's far more outgoing, and I think her feeling of self-worth has shot up."

Ta-Keesha urges other teens to volunteer as Big Brothers and Sisters. "You're that ray of sunshine that makes someone feel warm and good," she says. "It's great meaning something to somebody."

JULY 8, 1996, NORTHFIELD, MASS.

ta-keesha white

Sisters doing it for themselves: Ta-Keesha White, left, and Heidi Cyr.

photograph by julie bidwell

139

leigh-anne sastre

A lot of teens spend their after-school hours combing the refrigerator for leftovers. Not Leigh-Anne Sastre. She devoted her junior year at Foran High School in Milford, Conn., to a much more useful pursuit—scouring the neighborhood for pet chow.

Leigh-Anne, 17, had read an article about the Milford Animal Shelter's Pet-Food Bank and its efforts to fill the scrawny stomachs of underfed pets. So last year, as part of her Girl Scout activities, she decided to organize a pet-food drive. "There's always stuff being done for people," Leigh-Anne says, "but you hardly ever see food being collected for hungry animals."

She began with a letter-writing campaign, asking for donations from pet-food makers, retail stores, Girl Scout and Brownie troops, community groups, and churches. She sent out 200 letters and got a ton of responses. One-and-a-half tons, in fact—of pet food and supplies.

Most of the donors gave canned and dry food, the meat and potatoes of pet life. "But," says Leigh-Anne, "a lot of the little Brownies who helped me had very exotic minds. We received a cat toothbrush and toothpaste—something I'd never even heard of."

A local Brownie troop helped Leigh-Anne sort the donations and take them to the animal shelter. "It took two vans and a truck to get it all there," Leigh-Anne says. In just over a month, nearly all the supplies were gone, much of them given to low-income elderly owners of pets.

Leigh-Anne's efforts helped her win a Gold Award, the highest honor in Girl Scouts. After graduating from high school a year early, she's now at St. Joseph College in nearby West Hartford, studying to be a nurse.

The pet-food project is still going strong. "Last time I was at home," she reports, "I saw a Brownie collecting donations outside a local grocery store."

J U L Y   2 9 ,   1 9 9 6 ,   M I L F O R D ,   C O N N .

One thing Sylvie Davidson noticed in her history classes bothered her. "You read more about males than females," she says. "It wasn't just men who did the important things. There were women leading the way, too!"

Sylvie, 15, wanted to make kids aware of women's accomplishments. After a year of research and interviewing women, Sylvie wrote "From the Kitchen to the Assembly Line," a one-person skit about women who entered the work force during World War II. "There was a huge campaign to get women to work outside the home then," Sylvie says, "something that was unacceptable before the war except in certain fields, like teaching." Women were needed in factories to take the place of men who were in combat.

In her show, Sylvie introduces "Rosie the Riveter," a real woman who helped build airplane bombers at a Michigan factory in the early 1940s. Posters of Rosie were made to persuade women to join the work force. And millions did.

"Once women moved into the workplace, it was difficult to get them back home after the war," Sylvie says. "Some got a new sense of freedom from being able to support themselves. They found out that they could do the job just as well, if not better, than men."

Sylvie, a ninth-grader at Kingston Junior High in Poulsbo, Wash., took her show on the road to area elementary schools. Her 10-minute performance earned her a second place at the 1998 National History Day competition, a nationwide contest that encourages students to learn and share their knowledge of history. More than 600,000 teens competed last year.

"I like learning history through people's experiences," Sylvie says. "The on-the-job training women had during World War II was a huge step in helping women become equals in the workplace," she says. "And even though they're still working jobs similar to men but getting paid less, at least they're not stuck just doing housework."

MARCH 1, 1999, POULSBO, WASH.

sylvie davidson

143

ACKNOWLEDGEMENTS

There's

no greater joy for me than focusing on the positive. It is a great gift, for which I have many to thank, to be able to write each week of young people who are using their creative minds, their generous hearts and unbridled energy to help others.

First and foremost I would like to thank my husband, Carlo Vittorini, publisher of **react**. This empowering magazine for teenagers is his passion, and I see in his eyes his great care and concern each time I share a hero's story with him. I am deeply grateful to him and PARADE's editor, Walter Anderson, for creating **react** and allowing me to be a part of it. I am also grateful to S.I. Newhouse Jr., without whose support and encouragement **react** would not exist.

I would especially like to express my appreciation to the editor-in-chief of **react**, Lee Kravitz, who is the magazine's leader and visionary. Each time Lee says that "everyday heroes" reflects the spirit of the magazine, I'm inspired to dig deeper and search wider for all the many teens who should be recognized. I thank Lee and Susan Byrne, the managing editor, for their professional support and guidance, as well as their enthusiasm for my column. I'm also grateful to Rhonda Shafner, our research editor, who helps me hunt down names and phone numbers.

This collection of columns was Walter Anderson's idea and the work of several persons at PARADE magazine, our sister publication, including Dakila D. Divina, senior editor; Larry Smith, managing editor; Martin Timins, senior copy editor; and Ira Yoffe, director of design, who have devoted their talents to this book.

I'd also like to express my appreciation to Margaret Kemp and Melissa Spota of **react**'s photo department and to John Garvey and the PARADE production department. And what would I do without Esteban Haigler, who keeps my computer running?

To all the many friends and family who have helped me discover heroes, especially Helen Atkins, I say thank you...and, please, don't ever stop! And for your encouragement, understanding and the way you say, "I like your story, Mom," each time you read a new column, thank you, Frank and Ashley, my children and most-cherished gift. And to my parents, Jayne and Spencer Braddock, who taught me to always look for the best in life, my loving appreciation. Little did I know the best would be so easy to find.

—**Nancy Vittorini**